Global Business Guide:
How Small and Mid-Sized Companies
Grow beyond Borders

To my parents, Nezahat, Necdet Oge and to all Small and Mid-Sized Businesses bold enough to change the world.

Global Business Guide

Global Business Guide: How Small and Mid-Sized Companies Grow beyond Borders

Ultimate Trade LLC
5334 Lindley Avenue
Suite 324
Encino, CA 91316
Phone: 818-609-9196
http://www.goglobaltowin.com

Oge, Ayse

ISBN 978-0-615-22528-9
Business

Library of Congress Catalog

Printed in the USA
First Edition
First Printing October, 2008

Preface

Today's advancements in technology and communication have created enormous opportunities for small business to compete and thrive in international markets. This book helps remove fear of taking the plunge into the global arena without making costly mistakes. I wrote this book for those who said the following: "We have huge domestic market here, why go overseas. Going global is for large companies. International trade is too risky, hard to manage and not profitable." Globalization is here to stay. Small and medium-sized businesses need to respond with their unique ingenuity, creativity and innovation to make the most of global opportunities. Their export readiness and success, coupled with their job creation power, are crucial in leading us into the world economy.

This book is the result of eight years of experience (1970-1978) at CENTO (Central Treaty Organization), a political and economic international organization with member countries such as the United Kingdom, Pakistan, Iran and Turkey, and supporting member, United States based in Ankara and Turkey. Hands-on entrepreneurial experience as the owner of my own business; Marketing Professional working for Brenner International, a small Import Confectionery Company in North Hills, California; Corporate experience working for First Data, a leading Technology and Global Commerce Corporation, and finally my teaching and consulting experience at Long Beach City College with my 5-part Export Seminar, "Go Global to Win", to assist existing export firms in the development of the skills associated with successful exporting. What I drew out of my work experiences is that the international business environment nurtures growth and productivity as long as people are willing to learn and collaborate with each other. I also learned that small businesses are as capable as large companies to make a global impact.

"Global Business Guide" presents workable tools for business owners, managers, professionals and employees to take their companies into global arena. I have written this book to meet three objectives: (1) To encourage them to identify and take advantage of opportunities abroad, (2) To show resources that are available to them, (3) To share with them the basics of the international business. Whatever your company's tendencies and beliefs, starting and running a global operation can be exciting and extremely profitable. This book is intended to light the way, making the transition to profitable operation as short and painless as possible.

I am particularly indebted to extremely busy International Trade Professionals who took their time out to be interviewed. Qeun Mu Kim, President of U.S. Resource Recycling; Maurice Rasgon, Blue Cross Beauty Products, Inc; Fiona Taylor, Uniglobe Research Corporation; Joseph Martin, Bobrick; Bob Amudsen, Cardkey; Pascal Zandt, Meade; Ismail Maamoun, Anderco; Carol B Robinson, Calport Resources Inc; Peggy Randall, Artmaster Studios and Greg Mariscal, Hirsch Pipe.

Finally, I would like to thank Jane Kim, from University of Southern California, Annenberg School of Journalism, for her hard work and dedication to editing of the book.

Ayse Oge

Table of Contents

Global Selling Tips
Some Well Known International Mistakes
Styles of Presentation
New Global Thinking

Global Business Guide: How Small and Mid-Sized Companies Grow beyond Borders

Going Global:

Growth Opportunities
For Small and Mid-Sized Businesses

Today's evolutionary technology allows us to live in an integrated, interdependent and interconnected world. It creates enormous opportunities for small and mid-sized companies to compete and thrive in international markets. Small businesses have the advantage of being flexible, creative, ingenious and innovative. Since they are not cluttered with the layers of bureaucracy that their larger counterparts have, they move quickly through the decision-making process. The playing field in the international arena is leveled for small businesses to take the plunge – it lets them achieve growth and expansion and finally sharpen the competitive spirit of their owners and managers.

For many small companies, the important question is not *whether* to go global, but *how* to go global – that is, how to survive and prosper outside the narrow confines of a deceptively comfortable and familiar domestic market.

Some of the Incentives for Going Global are:

• Building sales and profits
When a company faces depressed sales in the local market, international markets can pick up the slack on low sales and achieve stability in revenues of the small business. Export managers know this well. As one Vice President who is involved in International Trade of a company, the leading supplier of material and equipment for cast polymer production based in Valencia, California indicated: "We

would be out of business if we had not gone global when the domestic market was extremely depressed," he says. "Sales are sales regardless where they are coming from." Export can help companies generate additional revenue in domestic downturns as well as during seasonal off-periods. For example, U.S. manufacturers of summer goods may do well in Australia during their summer period which coincides with our winter period. Counter marketing can even help out revenues and profits.

• Economic reason of going global

The U.S. Department of Commerce estimates that 95% of the world's population lives outside the U.S. and that two-thirds of the world's purchasing power is located overseas. If a small business is serious about competition and growth, it cannot afford to rule out the international marketplace. The plain truth is that the longer you are out of world markets, the more opportunities you lose and the more opportunities you give to your local and foreign competitors.

• Gaining competitive knowledge and ideas

Your presence in the overseas markets can also provide you with invaluable competitive information and know-how. Haagen-Dazs, the ice cream maker added a new flavor, "Dulche de Leche" to its line in Argentine in the late '90's. It was a caramelized milk flavor that became very popular in the Argentinean market. Haagen Daz later rolled out this winning item worldwide, and within less than a year it created $1 million in combined monthly revenues in the U.S. and Europe.

The vast majority of U.S. exporters are using their international operations as incubators for the next big hit. As the world is shrinking-the interchange and exchange of ideas are accelerated. Companies are reorganizing so that hot products from one region of the world can be more readily spotted and shipped elsewhere- either to U.S. or other international markets.

• Achieving economies of scale

When the demand increases by exports, a business can spread the fixed costs over a larger base of production. This will help them to reduce its unit costs and contribute to more profits.

• Technological advantage

If a firm has exhausted the distinct technological advantage of their product in the local market, the same product is a prime candidate for exports in countries that cannot afford high-priced items; or simply they would not need technologically advanced products.

• Unique products

Value-added niche products are very popular in world markets. Global consumers are looking for products that display performance, an appealing image and higher quality. Kenichi Ohmae, prominent globalization expert, indicates in his book "Going Global" that "when people make over $10,000 annual income, consumers purchasing habits, spending patterns are the same all over the world." Small businesses have a knack for filling these niches because they are flexible and have an extraordinary innovative advantage to produce products with speed. The enormous proliferation of microbreweries is a good example of niche marketing. People want a stronger, more particular flavor in their beer and are prepared to pay for it.

Niche products can be marketed as new or unique. What is new may be a twist on an old theme; as long as the idea is clearly attractive to the target audience, you are a winner. On the other hand, a brand-new product that does not fill a need in the global marketplace has very little chance to succeed, because novelty alone is not sufficient to drive sales.

With cutting-edge innovation, the product should be a technology-related line that is sparked by technological superiority, an attractive image and a perception of greater quality/value.

Brands with wide recognition internationally have significance in the hearts and minds of the global consumer. California has tremendous cache all over the world because of its pleasant climate and Hollywood glitz. The glamour and celebrity image of the movie industry causes it to be considered extremely valuable as an individual brand. Once, a California State University of Northridge Marketing Professor gave his keynote address at the 2002 Global conference held at Universal City, California. He met one of his foreign students who were making a decent profit in selling clothing to France and Italy. When the professor asked his student why he selected world fashion centers like Italy and France for his clothing line, the student's response was: "I am selling California to my distributors in Italy and France." California sportswear and outdoor-living trends are admired by foreign consumers abroad.

• **Website**

Once you have a website, you automatically own a global company. This can lead to buyers from abroad who are interested in your product and services visiting your site. But if you choose not to respond to the requests of prospective foreign buyers, you are ignoring new markets and losing potential revenue for your firm to grow and expand. The Web is the biggest tool to reach international markets with products that have global appeal.

• Free-Trade agreements

A world-wide trend towards free trade agreements is currently reflected by agreements such as the General Agreement on Tariffs and Trade (GATT), North American Free Trade Agreement (NAFTA), Central American Free Trade Agreement (CAFTA) and individual Free Trade Agreements between the U.S and Australia, Bahrain, Chile, Israel, Jordan, Morocco, Oman and Singapore. If we add free trade in the Eastern European countries, such as European Union and other emerging markets, small and mid-sized enterprises in the U.S. have a monumental chance to explore new markets and establish their global presence.

Emerging markets

In the mid-90's America was the dominant power of the world economy in terms of consumer spending. At the present time, emerging economies are reversing this trend and claiming leadership of world consumers by increasing spending by 65 percent.

Emerging markets in India, China, Mexico, Brazil, Argentina, South Africa, Poland, Turkey, Indonesia, Vietnam and South Korea are home to half of the world's population, and the United States exports more products to these countries than to Europe and Japan combined.

Key Selection Criteria:

- **They have large populations, vast resource bases and markets.**
  China, India and Indonesia are three of the four most populous countries in the world.

- **They are changing conventional economic order.**
  They are after larger global market share. They want to be equipped with the latest technology to be able to use their ingenuity to produce cutting edge and innovative products and services.

- **They are the world's fastest expanding markets.**
  They are striving very hard to climb the economic ladder, educating their workforces, focusing on technical research and building modern infrastructure.

- **They are in favor of free trade and market economy, to sell off their state enterprises.**

The pace of economic openness, entrepreneurial activity and existence of market economies in Argentina, India and Poland are impressive. All of these countries are important for U.S. exporters.

- **The big emerging markets have huge untapped potential.**

In most of the emerging markets, economic progress through international trade and investments was confined to selected regions, particularly large cities. China's expansion was centered on the southern coast. In Brazil, economic progress happened mainly in Sao Paulo, and in Indonesia, almost the entire modern business infrastructure was in Jakarta and its surrounding area. Economic progress in these countries is catching on to the "hinterlands", and this particular expansion trend presents an excellent opportunity for U.S. exporters.

In his book entitled "The New Asian Hemisphere," Mr. Mahbubani stated the following statistics as helpful for international trade professionals:

- In 2007, the developing countries produced over 52% of global growth, compared to 37% during the late 1990's.
- The percentage of total world output in the developing countries has risen to 29% in 2008 from 18% in 2005.
- By the year 2030, 361 million Chinese – more than the entire current population of the U.S. – may meet the World Bank's classification for middle class. This

includes the people who "buy cars, engage in international tourism, demand world-class products, and require international standards for higher education."

All of the facts mentioned above confirm that emerging markets provide huge growth opportunities for motivated and committed small and mid-sized American companies to market their products and services.

And if you add the emergence of a billion consumers from different parts of the world and the number of Internet users rising to three billion by the year of 2011 (stated by Silicon Valley Marketing Expert Tom Hayes in his book "Jump Point"), this will bring on a tough global competition. Small and mid-sized companies need to be well prepared to provide branded products and services to global consumers.

International Trade Strategy

Keys to global success

Exports have always been a good diversification of revenues and growth strategies for many existing businesses.

There are also costs and risks associated with exporting. It is critical to do a cost benefit analysis before you plan to export your goods/services. Some essential considerations to keep in mind are:

- Obtain qualified export counseling and put together a comprehensive international marketing plan before starting your export business. The plan should underscore your goals, objectives, and the challenges encountered.
- Secure a commitment from top management to overcome the initial difficulties and financial requirements of exporting. Think of international trade as a long term business and carefully monitor exporting efforts.
- Evaluate carefully all unsolicited inquiries.
- Devote continuous attention to export business when domestic business grows and thrives. Too many companies turn to exporting when local business falls in the United States.
- Treat international distributors and agents on an equal basis with domestic counterparts. Companies often carry out advertising campaigns, special discount offers, sales incentive programs, special credit term programs, and warranty offers in the U.S. market, but

fail to make similar offers to their international distributors.

- Print all service, sale, and warranty messages in locally understood languages. Although a distributor's top management may speak English, it is unlikely that all sales and service personnel have this capability.
- Provide servicing for the product. A product without the necessary service support can tarnish its reputation and brand quickly.

Evaluating a product's export potential

There are several ways to assess the overseas market potential of products and services. One of the most important ways is to evaluate the product's success in domestic markets. If a company does well in the U.S. market, there is a good chance that it will also be successful in markets abroad, wherever similar needs and conditions exist.

In markets that differ significantly from the U.S. market, some products may have limited potential. Several differences may be climate and environmental factors, social cultural factors, local availability of raw materials or product alternatives, lower wage costs, lower purchasing power, the availability of foreign exchange, and government import controls.

If a product is unique or has important features that are hard to duplicate abroad, chances of finding an export market are high. For a unique product, competition may be nonexistent or very slight, while demand may be quite high.

Deciding to go global

Once the company determines it has exportable products, it must still take into account other factors:

- What does the company want to gain from exporting?
- Is exporting consistent with other company goals?
- What demands will exports place on the company's key resources – management and personnel, production capacity, and finance – and how will these demands be met?

An important first step in planning is to develop a broad consensus among key management on the company's goals, objectives, capabilities, and constraints. The first time an export plan is developed, it should be kept simple. The initial planning effort itself generates more information and insights that can be included in more comprehensive planning documents later.

Preparing and selecting your products/services for exports

Selecting and preparing a product for export requires knowledge of the characteristics of each market being targeted. If the company manufactures more than one product or offers many models of a single product, it should start with the one best suited to the targeted market. Most of the companies select the product that requires no major design or engineering modifications. For starters who are new to the exporting business, the ideal countries consist of:

- International customers with the same demographics or products with the same specifications for manufactured goods.
- U.S. goods that needs no modifications.
- Products that can be sold on status or foreign appeal.
- Products that are sold on commodity or price basis.

Product adaptation

To enter a foreign market successfully, a U.S. company may have to modify its product to conform to government regulations, geographic and climatic conditions, buyer preferences, or standard of living. Detailed information on regulations imposed by foreign countries is available from the country desk officers of the Department of Commerce's District Office.

It is absolutely necessary for a firm to adapt its products to account for geographic and climatic conditions. Factors such as humidity, heat, and energy costs can affect the performance of a product or even define its use.

Buyer preference and purchasing habits in a foreign country may also lead U.S. manufacturer to modify its product. Local customs, such as religion or the use of leisure time, often determine whether a product will sell in a foreign country.

A country's standard of living can also determine whether a company needs to modify a product. The level of income, the level of education, and the availability of energy are determining factors of the potential acceptance of a product in foreign markets.

Market potential must be large enough to justify the direct and indirect costs involved in product adaptation. The firm needs to assess the costs and evaluate the benefits of global business and then figure out whether it would be worthwhile to sell the product overseas.

Engineering and redesign

Prospective exporters should be aware that even fundamental aspects of its products may require changing. For example, electrical standards in many foreign countries differ from U.S. electrical standards. The electrical standards sometimes vary even in the same country. By knowing the requirement, an exporter can come up with the right product that works in the foreign country.

Similarly, different kinds of equipment must be engineered in the metric system for integration with other pieces of equipment. Since the non-metric system is used in the U.S., exporters need to pay special attention to electrical measurements requirements adhered by the target foreign country. The exporter's instruction or maintenance manuals should include dimensions in centimeters, weights in grams or kilos, and temperatures in degrees Celsius. Information on foreign standards and certification systems is available from the National Center for Standards and Certificates Information, and the National Institute for Standards and Technology: http://www.nist.gov/.

Installation

Ease of installing is another consideration on the part of the exporter. The company should be careful to provide all product information in the local language, such as training manuals, installation instructions, and parts lists.

Servicing

Service after the sales is critical for some products; generally, the more complex the product technology, the greater the demand for pre-sale and post-sale service. Exporters tend to produce simple products that eliminate the need for costly maintenance and repairs in foreign countries. U.S. exporters who rely on a foreign distributor or agent to provide service backup must take steps such as training, periodically checking service quality, and monitoring inventories of spare parts.

Branding, labeling, and packaging

Consumers are concerned with both the product itself and the product's supplementary features, such as packaging, warranties, and service.

Some important branding considerations for the U.S. exporter:

- Are international brands well-known enough in the country to be exported? Should the exporter work on local or private labels to appeal to the local consumers?
- Are the colors used on labels and packages attractive or offensive to the foreign customers? For example, the color red means danger in the U.S., while the same color is good luck for Chinese people.
- Can labels be produced in the local language if required by law or practice?
- Does information on product content and country of origin have to be provided?
- Are weights and measures stated in the local unit?
- Must each item be labeled individually?
- Are local tastes and knowledge considered? A gift box picturing an American celebrity may not be as attractive to foreign customers as the picture of a local movie actor/actress.

Global branding

In the borderless economy based on commodity production, your brand can be the most important asset to set your product/service apart from competitors. Companies are moving from the price competition and relying more on the emotional punch that their brand offers to win consumers and maximize their sales and profits. Not long ago, Motorola was perceived by the consumers as a tech-driven seller of products, rather than a brand. The enormous success of RAZR, the ultra-light and thin cell-phone, changed Motorola's image and helped the company to position itself as a major consumer brand. The key to successful branding is creating the ultimate satisfying experience that the consumers remember by focusing on the look and feel of the product and not so much on the price.

Guidelines of building global brands:

- **Build a strong home base:**

Follow the rule of 80/20 by focusing on the needs and expectations of twenty percent of your local customers that provide the eighty percent of business.

- **Target the international competitive markets:**

Focus on entering foreign markets in which you can leverage your competitive advantages based on your core value, longevity in the business, market specialty, how your product is made, and leadership in product/service or technology.

- **Take advantage of co-branding and the foreign distributor's strength:**

Building your brand awareness in a foreign market thorough the co-branding strategy and distributor-established brands helps you to achieve early success. The distributors provide you with the customers and get the recognition you need to promote your products and services in a particular market.

• Niche marketing:

As you move into the consumer awareness phase in the foreign country, target the niche markets where there is little or no competition, and where you can find the most potential growth because your product/service has a strong appeal on the part of consumers.

• Go global act local:

Respect the cultural differences to make the emotional connection with the foreign audience.

• Appoint local companies to develop a culturally appropriate and sensitive marketing campaign:

A successful campaign needs to have a clear, defined objective and a powerful idea or icon that captures the imagination of the global customers.

Global branding gives you the edge in premium pricing, attracting co-branding, licensing opportunities, hiring the best employees and exercising power in any type of negotiations. In the global economy, almost everything can be commoditized; your brand is the only invaluable asset to win both local and foreign consumers.

Service Exports

Service industries range from fast food to high technology. The service sector accounts for about 70 percent of the U.S. GNP and 75 percent of overall employment.

The income generated and the jobs created through the sale of services abroad are just as important to the U.S. economy as income and jobs resulting from the production and export of goods. Those who have services to offer can become major participants in world trade.

Typical Service Exports

Services that are highly specialized, or technologically advanced and efficiently performed in the U.S are demanded in overseas markets. The following sectors have particularly high export potential:

- **Construction, design, and engineering.** The vast experience and technological leadership of the U.S. construction industry, as well as special skills in operations, maintenance, and management, give U.S. firms a competitive edge in international projects. Some U.S. firms have expertise in narrow niche fields, such as building earthquake proof buildings, power utilities and design, engineering services.

- **Banking and financial services.** U.S. financial institutions are very competitive all around the globe; particularly the ones that offer account management, credit card processing and risk assessment are at the forefront internationally.

- **Insurance services.** U.S. insurers offer services ranging from underwriting and risk evaluation to management contracts in the global marketplace.

- **Legal and accounting services.** Firms in this field aid other U.S. firms in legal and accounting activities. They also use their expertise to serve foreign firms in their business operations.

- **Teaching services.** Education services involve management, motivation speaking, sales training and the teaching of managerial and operational issues.

- **Management consulting services.** U.S. management consulting firms that are willing to sell their particular management skills find great potential buyers overseas.

Exporting services versus products

There are important features that differentiate exporting services from exporting products:

- Services are more intangible than products; therefore communicating a service offer is much more difficult than communicating a product offer. Suppliers of services need to pay attention to intangibility of a service to the prospective buyers.
- The intangibility of services makes financing difficult because it is hard to assess the end value of the service to the buyer.

- Selling services require personal interaction with the buyer and the seller has to be knowledgeable about cultural differences and nuances of the country he/she is targeting.
- Services are much harder to standardize than products. Service activities need to be adjusted to the needs and expectations of the customer.

Marketing services globally

Since majority of service exports are delivered in the support of product exports, service businesses can pair up with product exporters to take bundled goods/services to the international marketplace.

For service companies that are independent from products, they need to look to export markets that are similar to ones in the U.S or customize their services for that particular foreign market.

Once you make your decision to export your services abroad, make sure to contact the U.S. Department of Commerce and Commercial News USA to get exposure of your service worldwide.

The Eximbank has large scale programs that are aimed at U.S. construction, design, engineering, and architectural firms to assist in getting foreign contracts.

Evaluating your global alternatives

Methods of Exporting: Direct versus Indirect

Your decision on direct versus indirect exporting of your product is determined by several considerations:

- Control
- Resources in terms of people and capital
- Experience and knowledge in exporting
- Your product's requirement of on-site training and support.

If you want to keep the control of your export operation and have resources and experience in exporting, direct exporting would be your best alternative. Your product's on-site training and support needs would definitely require you to be where your customers are in order to cultivate a relationship and service them promptly.

Direct exporting

If you select direct exporting method, you as the owner of the company are responsible of the exporting operation, from finding customers to shipment of your product and collecting your money.

Advantage of direct exporting

- You have full control of export transactions.
- You know who your customers are.

- Your profits will be greater because you are eliminating intermediaries.
- You have a solid understanding of the market.

Disadvantages of direct exporting

- You need to invest time and money.
- Your company is responsible of every aspect of exports.

Indirect exporting is done through two intermediaries:

- Export Management Company
- Export Trading Company

Export Management Company

An Export Management Company serves like an extension of your company and is involved in the exporting of your product, collecting payment and coordinating the logistic of your shipments. An Export Management Company sells particular products to a well-defined customer base in a foreign country. For example, an EMC specializes in selling casual clothing to wholesalers in Europe; they buy the product from the manufacturer and sell it to the customer at a profit.

An EMC is an exporter and actively promotes your product in one or more countries, and it supposedly has expertise in specific markets and types of products.

It carries non-competing lines in the same broad product category which allows them to make the most of their investment in travel expenses, time and overhead.

An EMC has an established network of overseas agents to promote your product abroad, which saves you time and money in the long term.

Before you decide to hire an EMC, you need to determine what your export's needs and expectations are and check their references to find the most suitable one for your company.

An EMC is responsible for export transactions in locating markets and finding customers for your product, arranging agents and distributors, negotiating with the buyers and shipping, and showing your product at international trade shows.

Main sources to locate an EMC are:
- U.S. Export Assistance Centers of U.S. Department of Commerce
- Yellow Pages
- Chamber of Commerce
- Freight Forwarders
- Local trade Association with international focus

Export Trading Company

Export Trading Companies function on a demand basis. Demand of a specific product leads them to locate suppliers in the local market. For example, an ETC may get a request from a customer to purchase canned tuna fish, and they look for a supplier that can supply ten containers load of tuna fish every month for seven months with the best price and quality.

Regardless of whether you are selling direct or indirect, your customers will most likely be an overseas agent or representative, a distributor or importing wholesaler, an overseas end-user or a trading company.

Making the overseas connection

Many U.S. exporters entered the global marketplace in response to a request from an interested foreign firm. Usually foreign letters of inquiry are in English. If they aren't, most of the banks and freight forwarders can help you with translation, or you can use the services of a translator or go to the foreign language department of a local college or university.

Typically an inquiry covers the request of product specifications, approximate delivery time, and price; in some cases, they may want to know about shipping costs, terms and exclusivity arrangements. Some foreign firms are interested in buying for internal use while others (such as distributors/agents) are interested in buying to re-sell. A few firms may know your firm and be familiar with your products and want to place an immediate order. When you receive foreign inquiries about your product/service, here are some steps to take:

- Set up a foreign inquiry file and reply promptly, completely and clearly for all inquiries. Even if the inquiry is from a company that is familiar with your company, make sure to include a short introduction about you, your firm and your products, including your bank references, information on cost, delivery terms and required method of payment.
- Send your reply by e-mail, fax or air mail.
- Check the legitimacy of the inquiry. Sources are: business libraries, publications such as Dun and Bradstreet's Principal International Business and other

regional and country directories. International banks are good sources of information on the financial condition of firms located in foreign countries and the Commercial section of most foreign embassies have directories of firms located in their respective countries.

If you want to proactively pursue new customers abroad, tapping into your existing network of colleagues, suppliers, banks and associates will help you generate valuable leads. We are usually much more resourceful than we think; you may be the supplier to a foreign-based company that has customers in its home country. Or you may be outsourcing products/services for your operation from abroad. These are the primary contacts that you need to focus on diligently and have them introduce you to warm leads that you can build relationships with over time.

Overseas agent or representative

An overseas agent or importer works on 5-10 percent commission when locating buyers for your product. Once a buyer is found, the exporter is responsible for customer service and all transaction logistics, including setting up payment and arranging transportation. Most of the time prices quoted to the customer include the agent's commission. The agent oversees your work and stays in close contact with the customer. In many countries the agents are considered as your employees and if you try to terminate them, they are protected by their respective country's agency laws. In your contracts, try to refer to them as your representatives as opposed to agents because the procedure is much easier to terminate.

Distributor

A distributor buys the product from you, takes the title of the goods and marks up a profit between 25-35 percent. Distributor then warehouses, distributes and re-sells them to the customer.

A distributor takes care of after-sales service, advertises products in different media and exhibits at trade shows and provides financing for customers.

Most distributors want to work on an "exclusive basis only" in certain territories and carry complementary products. For example, if they carry wafer and cookie lines, your candy can be a perfect match for them to sell to their customers. Once you locate a good distributor that can carry out your export function, set up a contractual agreement for a period of one year and monitor his/her sales performance and see how things work out between you and him. You can always extend your agreement if you reach a win-win relationship.

When evaluating prospective distributors you should look for the following requirements:
- Trade in the area you want to sell.
- Experience in importing, marketing and promoting your type of product.
- Distribute products similar to yours but that are non-competing.
- Have financial stability.
- Have integrity and honesty.

Regardless how you want to structure your export operations to achieve the best result from overseas sales, take small steps and learn as you go along and integrate exports into your local business. Some golden rules are:

- Don't rush taking on large sections or portions of the world.
- Avoid long range commitments.
- Be flexible, things change constantly.
- Take a serious interest in overseas markets.
- Develop relationships with intermediaries, buyers and customers.
- Put everything in writing.
- Conduct due diligence on current and potential distributors.

Guidelines in granting exclusivity to distributors:

- Put together contracts on the basis of realistic performance clauses that allows you to escape the agreement if the distributor non-performs.
- Structure contract in such a way that all performance targets are stated numerically.
- Grant gradual exclusivity to your distributors that represent you overseas and earn your business.
- Exclusivity based on a territory – For example, if you have a distributor working in Greece, Turkey and Egypt. Start granting exclusivity with one country as opposed to three of them at once.
- Exclusivity based on a product – For example, if you have a technology to decontaminate water and filter system. Start exclusivity with filter system. If the distributor produces consistent sales, you may consider giving exclusivity on technology as well.
- Exclusivity based on sales outlets– For example, if you have medical equipment that can be sold in nursing homes, hospitals and pharmacies, grant exclusivity only in one sales outlet. If distributor achieves

satisfactory production for example in one sales outlet, pharmacies, you can also consider giving exclusivity to her/him for others.

It takes patience and perseverance to develop long term relationships. There is a lot of trust and saving face involved in overseas business. Your success depends on how you want to strategize exports. If your company is strong in local sales; anything that you sell overseas will be an additional revenue stream, and it also gives a chance to lower your costs by expanding your production. International business provides you with exposure to competitive knowledge and trends, and helps you stay ahead of your competitors.

Sources to locate and identify potential distributors and agents

- U.S. Export Assistance Center, U.S. Department of Commerce
- Agent/Distributor Services
- Gold Key Program
- Commercial News U.S.A
- Web Sites
- Stat-USA (www.stat.usa.org)
- Trade Port (www.tradeport.org)
- World Trade Centers
- Commercial Banks
- Foreign Freight Forwarders

The best way to locate agents and distributors is to travel to the target country and meet your end users and customers face to face, and to ask for recommendations on the people who are selling them. Trade shows are great venues to meet Distributors and Agents. The best shows are held in Europe, particularly Consumers Product show in Germany. Allied but non-competing product manufacturers can recommend you agents/distributors as well.

Overseas retailer

You can sell your products directly to overseas retailers, such as department stores, supermarkets or mail-order houses on either exclusive or non-exclusive basis. Since they are small and service a limited location, your products have limited exposure.

Overseas end-users

You can market your products directly to certain types of end-users, such as hospitals, universities or original equipment manufacturers.

Other ways of establishing international presence

Licensing

A foreign firm can license your patents, trademarks, copyrights or know-how for an agreed-upon fee to be paid as a lump sum or as royalties over time. The fees are established and negotiated based on volume, intended use, period of use and other factors. Licensing technology can help the licensor make a much more rapid and complete entry into a foreign market. At the same time, such an agreement reduces the financial and legal risk of owning and operating a foreign manufacturing facility or taking part in an overseas venture.

Licensing can be appealing to small companies that do not have extensive foreign trade experience and infrastructure to enter successfully into such markets on their own. Over the last decade, some U.S candy manufacturers and California fashion designers have been selling their products to the world's savvy customers through licensing agreements.

Some technology companies find licensing an attractive option when they sell outdated technology in the home country to foreign countries.

Licensing has drawbacks too. It shifts the international marketing functions to the licensee. And some licensee's may lack the expertise and marketing knowledge to penetrate the market. A more serious drawback lies in the event that the licensor may create its own competitor, both in the markets the agreement was made, where they have low wage structure to manufacture the product in less expensive way and in other potential export countries.

Trademark licensing

Trademark licensing has become a substantial source of worldwide revenue for companies that own well-known brands, logos and distinctive images. Trademark licensing is common on clothing, games, foods and gifts and novelties. And the licensor enjoys free services of walking advertisement and wide exposure generated by the consumption of other products.

Trademarks are used on different but congenial product category. For example, Laura Ashley's name on furniture is aimed at winning over the customers who like an aura of casual elegance in clothing style.

Franchising

International franchising has grown tremendously. It can be an extremely effective way of establishing presence in the foreign market. Foreign governments tend to look favorably on franchising because it does not replace exports or export jobs.

Joint ventures

Joint ventures have become a standard business practice in international trade. Joint ventures are common in service related businesses and manufacturing.

Many U.S firms prefer joint ventures because it reduces the high cost of getting established in the areas of manufacturing, distribution and marketing. The potential problem occurs when the U.S firm loses management control to its partner. This may result in high costs, or a mediocre quality of product.

Once you decide to take the joint ventures option to expand your company's presence globally, it is important to get leads and advice from local reputable legal and accounting firms in your area. Visiting and interviewing the executives of the foreign firm will give you ample ammunition to find out whether there will be a right match between your firm and theirs in terms of business philosophy, shared values and a complementary knowledge base.

Common Mistakes

Some of the common mistakes new exporters make are:
- Failure to understand the import regulations of your target markets.
- Demonstrating poor judgment in selecting overseas sales representatives or distributors. It is best to interview couple of qualified reps and to check their past performance to judge whether they will be the right people for your business.
- Trying to consider a wide range of countries to export rather than concentrating on one or two geographical areas and establishing a basis for profitable operations and solid growth.
- Assuming that the same marketing, promotional or advertising tools will be successful in each foreign market. For example, Pepsi's popular advertising slogan in the United States; "Come Alive with the Pepsi Generation" was translated into Chinese as "Pepsi brings your ancestors back from the grave" was not welcomed in China.
- Unwillingness to modify products to meet local safety and cultural norms.

Technology is your best ally in connecting with your counterparts. The internet, videoconferencing and mobile phones make it possible for small business to be in several countries at once. Going global offers great opportunities for small and medium-sized businesses; it makes your size irrelevant and allows you to showcase your creativity, flexibility and most importantly, your determination.

Tapping into powerhouses of help

Small and Medium-Sized businesses are not alone in their export journey; there is tremendous assistance on the part of the following organizations:

- The Small Business Administration and Small Business Development Centers offer export consultation at their offices throughout the country. The centers utilize the expertise of consultants and trainers who have hands-on experience in exports.
- The U.S. Export Assistance Centers (USEAC's) combine the services of the Department of Commerce (DOC), the Export-Import Bank, and the Small Business Administration all under one umbrella. This group provides excellent training seminars for prospective exporters. The training is done by competent exporters from the industry; staff from DOC, attorneys specialized at international law, and personnel from Service Corps of Retired Executive (SCORE) and the SBA. They also provide an Export Working Capital Program for experienced exporters that have contracts and Letters of Credit with foreign buyers.
- Foreign Embassies and Consulates can be of help to small businesses by guiding their research. They have knowledgeable staff that is in a position to give you specific information tailored to your needs.
- Freight Forwarders and Custom Brokers can be the right arm of small businesses when it comes to advice on export laws and regulations.
- Major international carriers such as FedEx, UPS and DHL have customized services for exporters to make their export venture cost-effective. **FedEx Global**

Manager helps you with international documents for your shipment, estimates duties and taxes, and finally gets critical regulatory and country information about your target country. **UPS TradeAbility** program enables your company to effectively manage the movement of goods across international borders in a compliant, prompt and efficient manner. **DHL** provides Worldwide Priority and International Document Service, Import Express and DHL Global Mail and Forwarding.

Cardkey, a company of 300 employees based in Simi Valley, California, specializes in access control cards and does business in Australia, India, Korea and South America. The Export Manager of Cardkey, Bob Amundsen, says that "developing alliances with **UPS**, **Federal Express**, **DHL** is extremely important for small companies. Since they are on top of all the laws of the importing country, all they need from you most of the time is a Commercial Invoice or Certificate of Origin and they do the rest."

Bob also points out the following: "Sometimes the shipping is 'Airport to Airport'. In such cases, the small business supplies only the necessary paperwork and the carrier will take it to the Customs Office in the importing country where the end-user will pick up the shipment. These arrangements provide enormous savings to small businesses since direct shipping eliminates all middleman costs."

Department of Commerce: Your Partner in Global Business

The local Department of Commerce, which houses the U.S. Export Assistance Center (USEAC), the International Trade Administration (ITA) and the US Foreign Commercial Services (US&FCS), runs a series of programs to put exporters and their prospective customers in touch.

- **Matchmakers Service**
  Matchmakers Service introduces beginner export companies to motivated agents, distributors and large retailers through DOC or ITA.

- **Gold Key Program**
  For a small company with an export budget, the Gold Key Program is perfect, as it allows the company to meet with a pre-screened agent, distributor or a joint venture partner. Individual meetings arranged by the Commercial Officers take place at the U.S. Embassy in the host country.

Gold Key Program is a great investment on the part of small business. For example, Rocket Man, a very small business and provider of portable beverage dispensing products, got into export marketing in the early 1990's with the help of the Louisville, Kentucky office of the U.S. Department of Commerce. Exports have been instrumental for the company to expand its distribution to 35 countries including Austria, Mexico, Canada, Brazil and Portugal within three years. They also diversified their product lines to include pre-mixed beverages and a hot water heating system. Export sales have been an engine of growth for Rocket Man, it became the fastest growing exporter in

Kentucky, and has been written up and recognized by numerous publications for its rapid expansion.

- **Trade Missions**
  Trade missions are designed to assist beginner exporters in establishing sales and setting up representation abroad at a low cost. The organizer of the mission sets up the itinerary, which covers travel arrangements, appointments with prospective customers and opportunities to feel out the market and other trade intermediaries for your products.

- **Catalog and Video Exhibitions**
  U.S. companies can have their sales literature or videos displayed at U.S. embassies abroad, as well as the appropriate trade shows, where they will be seen by prospective distributors, agents and other interested buyers.

- **Agent Distributor Service (ADS)**
  Agent Distributor Service finds qualified distribution firms that are currently handling products similar to yours. An ADS search can generate up to six names of distributors who have an interest in specific U.S. products.

- **Export Contact List Service**
  List service generates a mailing list of potential importers for your product from the Department of Commerce's automated global network of overseas firms.

- **Economic Bulletin Board (EBB)**
  The Economic Bulletin Board provides online trade leads, time sensitive market information and the latest statistical releases from a variety of federal agencies.

- **International Company Profile**
  U.S. Commercial Service can provide you with customized reports that evaluate potential or existing trading partners. Reports include background information, reputation and credit-worthiness.

- **Commercial News USA**
  You can advertise in Commercial News USA, a monthly catalog-magazine that provides global exposure for products and services that are ready to export. The free magazine is mailed directly to qualified recipients and distributed by U.S. and Foreign Commercial Service personnel at U.S. embassies and consulates worldwide.

Recreatives, a Buffalo-based manufacturer of all terrain motor vehicles and recreational equipment, relies exclusively on Commercial News USA to help it find new markets overseas. "We dabbled in exporting with sporadic success in the early days of the company." Reich, the Marketing Director, says. "But we didn't have much continued success until we started advertising in Commercial News USA. For about 10 years, our sole source of international marketing was Commercial News USA."

In recent years, the Internet also has provided a big sales boost. "It amplifies our print advertising, and we now get better results because of e-commerce," says Reich. "The print ads and the Internet complement each other because the print drives customers to our Web site." Recreatives' export markets are Eastern Europe, Russia, Guatemala, Chile, Argentine, Brazil and Honduras.

The retail prices for Recreatives' vehicles range from $5,785 to $13,995. Exporting has proven lucrative for Recreatives because international customers tend to order the company's higher-end, higher margin models that use Kawasaki engines. Founded in 1969, Recreatives Industries began exporting in 1985. Since then, the export sales have been increasing over 10% each year.

Certified Trade Fair Program

The Department of Commerce's Foreign Buyer Program certifies a specific number of U.S. trade shows each year. For small and medium-sized trade businesses, trade shows are a cost-effective solution to meet prospective buyers and get your company's name out there.

The U.S. Department of Commerce has put together the Certified Trade Fair Program for small companies that are new to exporting opportunities to be acclimated in international markets and locate overseas buyers. The Department of Commerce selects the right event for prospective exporters and extends assistance in freight forwarding, customs clearance, exhibit designing and setup, public relations, and comprehensive show promotion and marketing.

Advantages of Exhibiting at Trade Shows are:
- Accomplish own marketing research and collect competitive information about your industry
- Achieve high visibility for your company and products

- Meet sales agents, brokers, importing trading companies, distributors, independent sales reps and government officials in the local market

The Federation of International Trade Associations offers websites with its trade show listings:
www.fita.orga/shows.html
www.goevents.com
www.expoworld.net

The Commerce Department and its trade arm, Commercial Service, can help you get established. The U.S. Chamber of Commerce has offices in cities all over the world. Most states have economic development agencies with international trade offices. All are ready to help you find distributors, trading partners and other leads.

The U.S. Department of Commerce offers free, individual export counseling at more than 60 U.S. Export Assistance Centers across the country.

For the Center nearest you, call 1-800-872-8723 or visit www.export.gov.

International Business is a Team Effort

Once small business owners, get established and start getting orders from foreign prospects, they need to surround themselves with a capable and professional team of people who are specialized in international trade and can help in every step of the way. Your team should consist of:

- Insurance Broker
- Attorney
- Accountant
- Banker
- Freight Forwarder/Custom Broker

Insurance Broker handles your export insurance needs. Export Credit Insurance is protection against a foreign customer's failure to pay you. Credit insurance encourages the use of competitive selling terms while providing a critical protection against default of payment. Insured receivables can also be used as loan collateral when obtaining additional financing.

Covering your key person through a best man insurance who handles your export operation is important to have uninterrupted global business.

Attorneys specialized in international trade can help you get fair agreements when you are conducting business with your foreign counterparts. You can check services of Bar Association in your area and interview them in your initial consultations to make sure that you will communicate well in the future.

A good accountant can help maximize your cash flow, put money back into your company and protect you from double taxation.

Banker can assist you to finance an export sale, guide you in putting together competitive terms, and advise you on the risk factor.

Freight Forwarders and Custom Brokers are instrumental in moving your freight domestically and internationally. Some freight forwarders and custom brokers have experience in certain countries and specific products. What you should look for in freight forwarders are reputation, knowledge and experience in your product, as well as a service relationship with carriers. If the freight forwarder can help you get the product in the hands of your customer who is located at a remote location and at a very short notice; you will have that customer for life. The best source in locating freight forwarder is through the Foreign Trade Association.

Market Research

Market research includes all methods that a company uses to find out which foreign markets have the best potential for its products. A firm may research foreign markets by using either primary or secondary data resources.

Primary research involves collecting data directly from the foreign marketplace through interviews, surveys and other direct contacts with reps and potential buyers. The advantage of primary research is it can be customized based on the needs of foreign customers and provides answers to specific questions. The downside of this type of research is that it's extremely time-consuming and expensive.

Working with secondary sources is less expensive and helps the company focus its marketing efforts. Major limitations of this type of research are that the data can be old, or product breakdowns may be too broad to be of much value to a company. Statistics on the service sector are often unavailable, but some statistics are misleading. For example, one statistic states that large amounts of certain goods were exported to a Panamian free port. The reality is that most of these goods are intended for re-export to other countries in Central and South America.

Another pitfall in statistical analysis occurs when the product you propose to export is not defined by the ten-digit HS (Harmonized System). In this event it is necessary to extrapolate by checking the broader definition to determine if this general type of product is being imported by a given country or region, and let the remainder of your country research reinforce any tentative assumptions.

Step by Step Approach to Market Research
Screen potential markets

- Obtain export statistics that indicate product exports to various countries.
- Identify five to ten large and fast-growing markets for your product. Determine how consistent markets are in terms of imports.
- Look for smaller and quickly-emerging markets that may provide ground floor opportunities.

Study Target Markets

Step One
- Examine trends that can influence demand.
- Calculate overall consumption of the products and the amount accounted for by imports.

Step Two
- Who is your target market?
- Size of the market and competition.

Criteria in Selecting Target Market
- **Volume Potential** – Your goal is to seek the highest sales with the least investment, promotion and manpower.
- **High Market Share** – If U.S. exports have a significant market share at target markets, you have an advantage there.
- **Location** – You can save travel time and expenses if you focus on countries in close proximity.

Step Three
Analyze your data in terms of demand, channels of distribution, cultural differences and business practices.

Step Four
Identify both foreign barriers (tariff or non tariff) and U.S. barriers for the product being imported.
After analyzing the data, focus on countries that will be most cost-effective for your company to export overseas.

Harmonized System

Trade transactions are classified under the Harmonized System leaving the U.S. The HS number must be used when completing the Shippers Export Declaration Form. You can contact the nearest U.S. Export Assistance Center to obtain your HS number or you can buy HS CD-ROM of Department of Commerce.

Sources of Data

- Call 1-800-USA-TRADE to find trade specialist and get answers to your export questions.
- Go to the website:
  http://www.export.gov/mrktresearch/index.asp
- Check the latest trade statistics at http://tse.export.gov/

Government

You can visit or call Trade Attaches or Commercial Counselor to obtain data on that particular country.

- **International Organizations**

International organizations provide data for exporters. Some useful websites are:

- The World Bank Atlas published by World Bank, which provides data on population, growth trends and GNP figures.
  www.worldbank.org
- The World Trade Organization
  www.wto.org
- Organization for Economic Cooperation and Development, which publishes annual and quarterly reports on member countries.
  www.oecd.org
- Monetary Fund
  www.imf.org

Service Organizations

Banks, accounting firms, international trade consultants and freight forwarders can be a great source for research material.

Trade Associations

Domestic and international chambers of commerce can provide you with invaluable information.

National Trade Data Bank

National Trade Data Bank is a very comprehensive research tool that focuses on global trade outlook, country commercial guides, sales outlets such as distributors and agents, and even provides contacts of foreign buyers interested in U.S. products or services and upcoming trade shows. NTDB can be accessed by local and college libraries, or you can also subscribe for a nominal fee.

Other Federal Export Assistance Resources

- Export-Import Bank of the United States (Ex-Im Bank)
- Local Colleges and Universities
- Internet
- Foreign Embassies and Consulates

Alibaba, E-Commerce Company

Alibaba.com, is the world's leading business to business e-commerce company. Alibaba provides an efficient, trusted platform connecting small and mediums sized buyers and suppliers from around the world. Company's international marketplace (www.alibaba.com) focuses on global importers and exporters and the China marketplace (www.alibaba.com.cn) covers suppliers and buyers trading domestically in China. Together Alibaba's marketplace forms a community of close to 30 million registered users from 240 countries and regions.

The company's headquarters is based in Eastern China. Alibaba has field sales and marketing offices in more than 30 cities in China, Hong Kong, Switzerland and the United States.

Trade Compliance Publications

U.S. Customs & Border Protection has a number of Informed Compliance Publications (ICPs) in the "What Every Members of the Trade Community Should Know About" series. Three publications titles of general interest are:

- What Every Member of the Trade Community Should Know About Recordkeeping
- What Every Member of the Trade Community Should Know About Rules of Origin
- What Every Member of the Trade Community Should Know About Foreign Assembly of the U.S.

To download these documents, visit http://www.cbp.gov/xp/cgov/toolbox/legal/informed_compliance_pubs/.

Global Pricing

Price is an important factor in a buyer's decision and serves as a penetration and positioning tool in international marketing. Price is the only element of marketing mix that generates revenue, as all other elements are costs.

First-Time Pricing

You need to consider the following principles when you are working on your first time pricing:
- Skimming

The objective of skimming is to achieve the highest possible contribution in a short time. The product has to be unique, and a large segment of the market must be willing to pay the high price. You can identify a potential market segment during the market research. If the competition may duplicate your product, fast skimming is not the best tactic.

- Market Pricing

If similar products already exist in the target market, the standard approach you need to adopt is market pricing. The final customer price is based on competitive pricing, and then production and marketing expenses must be adjusted to the price.

- Penetration Pricing

Penetration pricing means low prices are aimed at generating high volume and market share. It requires mass markets, price sensitive customers and the capacity to reduce production and marketing costs as volume increases.

As a rule of thumb, exporters take 10% -15% markups over cost, which is the price a manufacturer charges you when you buy a product from them. For example, if your supplier charges you $1.00 per unit for his product, you might mark it up anywhere from $1.10 to $1.15 per unit. This markup is your profit.

Three Ways to Determine Export Pricing

- **Rigid Cost-Plus**

You can set export prices three to four percent higher than domestic prices to cover the cost of foreign advertising, travel and shipping

- **Flexible Cost-Plus**

You can offer special discounts to gain market share and offset exchange rate fluctuations

- **Dynamic Incremental**

You may adjust prices day to day as dictated by the exchange rate.

Export License

Before you contact a freight forwarder, check if you need an Export License for your product. A validated export license is assigned to a specific exporter for a specific product, either for a designated period of time or for a single transaction. The following types of products are subjected to export licenses:

- Goods that pose potential harm to your own country's security
- Goods that cause a shortage in your own country

- Goods that affect your country's foreign policy

You can get the following form at the Bureau of Export Administration: BXA-622P, Application for Export License. Once it is filled out, submit it to the BXA.

When you are working on your quotation, you must contact a freight forwarder who will provide you with a shipping rate. Fees are determined by the following:
- Shipping your product by air or by ocean?
- Tariff on your product
- Amount of traffic to and from your destination point.
- Exchange rates

When your freight forwarder provides with you a quote, total charges are broken down by:
- Inland transport: moving expense from a factory door to a port of exit within the same country
- Ocean or air transport
- Currency Adjustment Factor

Documentation and freight forwarder's fee for handling all documentation with shipment, and letters of credit

Terms of Shipment
- **CIF (cost, insurance and freight)**
Seller is responsible for paying the freight and insurance in advance.
- **CFR (cost and freight)**
Seller is responsible for paying the freight costs and collecting from customer later.
- **FAS (free alongside ship)**
Seller is responsible to get the goods shipside, ready to be loaded, and pay all the costs to that point. Customer is

responsible for the cost of loading the goods into port at the specified place.

- **FOB (Free on Board)**

Seller must take care of all paperwork and/or expenses necessary to collect the goods from the supplier and place them on an international carrier.

- **Ex (Ex Factory or Ex Dock)**

Terms beginning with "Ex" indicate that the price quoted to your customer applies only at the specified point of origin (you or your supplier's factory, or a dock at the export point).

Ways of Checking Foreign Customers Credit Worthiness

- **Exporters**

You can check your buyer's credit-worthiness through firms within your industry

- **Commercial Banks**

You can ask your Account Manager for a confidential financial report on each foreign firm seeking credit terms

- **Dun and Bradstreet**

D&B provides "International Business Information Reports" on firms located in foreign countries. Their website is: www.dnb.com.

- **Ex-Im Bank**

Their website is: www.exim.gov.

- **World Trader Data Report**

The Data Report is a government report that contains information from the U.S. Embassy or Consulate located in the country of the potential buyer. You can request this report through the nearest District Office of the U.S. Department of Commerce.

Access to Capital for Global Business Export Finance Programs for Small and Medium-Sized Companies

Banks are often more willing to lend money to a small exporter if the company has a guarantee of payment from a state or federal agency. Such guarantees eliminate a bank's risk if the exporter defaults. Guarantees may be obtained from the Small Business Administration or the Export-Import Bank.

Also large banks nationwide have intensified their efforts in the export area. They provide letters of credit, foreign-exchange services, and working capital to fund the production of goods for export.

The U.S., Small Business Administration (SBA) offers a variety of financing services for exporters. They include international trade loan programs, an export working-capital guarantee program which provides short-term financing for individual, business loan-guarantee program for medium-working capital and long-term fixed-asset financing. To reach SBA:
1-800-U-ASK-SBA (800-827-5722)
http://www.sba.gov/

The Export-Import Bank, an independent federal agency, offers a working-capital guarantee program that covers hundred percent of the amount of a commercial loan. The agency also offers an export credit insurance program to protect exporters in case their foreign buyer defaults on payment. To reach Exim Bank:
202-565-3946 or 800-565-3946
http://www.exim.gov/

The Small Business Administration Export Working Capital Program supports export financing to small businesses when that financing is not otherwise available on reasonable terms. The program encourages lenders to offer export working capital loans by guaranteeing repayment of up to $1 million or 90 percent of a loan amount, whichever is less. A loan can support a single transaction or multiple sales on a revolving basis.

SBA Export Express helps small businesses that have exporting potential, but need funds to buy or produce goods, and/or provide services, for export.

Eligibility Requirements;
- Meet SBA's size standards for small businesses
- Have been in business for at least 12 continuous months
- All types of businesses considered, including service exporters
- Businesses not directly exporting, but produce or sell product/services for export

Mr. Qeun Mu Kim, President of U.S. Resource Recycling, Inc. based in Fontana, California, received an SBA-guaranteed loan in the form of an Export Working Capital Loan in excess of $750,000 to fuel business expansion. The loan provided funds that allowed Kim to add crushing and compression equipment, and to generate cash flow in the purchase of materials. Kim says he does not know how he could have managed growth without the assistance of the SBA and its loans.

Finding an export niche market was Kim's goal when he launched a program to expand U.S. Resource Recycling Inc., which originally started out with 26 employees, into a larger foreign market. U.S. Resource Recycling purchases materials such as paper products, which are then recycled and sold as exports in the company's primary markets, including South Korea, Japan, Taiwan and China. Kim found that more primary users of waste paper in foreign markets were willing to pay a premium for the product compared with customers in U.S. markets.

Kim now communicates with and sells directly to the consumers in the overseas markets. He often finds that subsidiary buyers and distributors pass added costs onto the end-user. However, Kim avoids pass-along costs incurred by several steps of middlemen, and he can sell the product at a fair price to earn more income for his business.

A domino effect takes place, and the higher fees Kim collects allow him to pay higher prices for raw materials purchased in the U.S., and build a sufficient inventory to appeal to the overseas buyer seeking to purchase in greater volume. As part of his marketing efforts, Kim purchases a higher-quality waste paper and employs a sorting process to offer "best quality" paper.

Getting paid and playing safe in global business

Methods of Payment

There are several basic methods of receiving payment for products sold abroad. Ranked in order of most secure to least secure, the basic methods of payment are:

- Cash in advance
- Letter of credit
- Documentary collection or draft
- Open account

Since getting paid in full and on time is of utmost concern to exporters, risk is a major consideration. Many factors make exporting riskier than domestic sales. Exporters are advised to consult an international banker to determine an acceptable payment for each specific transaction.

Cash in advance

Cash in advance before shipment is the "gold standard" in commerce. Sellers can always ask for "cash in advance" and definitely should demand it for small trial orders of less than $10,000.

If a supplier is customizing the product for customer, he/she must be paid the initial expenses up front.

Cash in advance is a good option when sellers have the slightest doubt about a customer's ability to pay for the goods/services. On the other hand, advance payment creates cash flow problems and increases risks for the buyer, who may refuse to pay until the merchandise is received.

Documentary letter of credit and drafts

The buyer may be concerned that the goods will not be sent if the payment is made in advance. To protect the interests of both buyer and seller, documentary letters of credit or drafts are often used. Under these two methods, documents are required to be presented before the payment is made. Both letters of credit and drafts may be paid immediately, at sight, or at a later date. Drafts that are to be paid when presented for payment are called "sight drafts." Drafts that are to be paid at a later date, which is often after buyer receives the goods, are called "time drafts" or "date drafts."

Letters of credit

A letter of credit adds a bank's promise of paying the exporter to that of the foreign buyer when the exporter has complied with all of the terms and conditions of the letter of credit. The foreign buyer applies for issuance of a letter of credit to the exporter and therefore is called the applicant; the exporter is called the beneficiary.

Payment under a documentary letter of credit is based on documents, not on the terms of sale or the condition of the goods sold. Before payment, the bank responsible for making the payment verifies that all documents are exactly as required by the letter of credit. When a discrepancy exists, it must be corrected before payment can be made. The full compliance of documents with those specified in the letter of credit is mandatory.

A letter of credit may be either irrevocable (it cannot be changed unless both the buyer and the seller agree to make the change) and banks pay even default happens; or revocable (either party may unilaterally make changes) and bank does not pay if customer defaults.

Drafts

A draft, sometimes also called a bill of exchange, is similar to a foreign buyer's check. Like checks used in domestic commerce, drafts sometimes carry the risk that they will be dishonored.

Sight Drafts

A sight draft is used when the seller wishes to retain their title to the shipment until it reaches its destination and is paid for.

Time drafts and Date Drafts

If the exporter wants to extend credit to the buyer, a time draft can be used to state that the payment is due within a certain time after the buyer accepts the draft and receives the goods; for example, 30 days after acceptance. By signing and writing "accepted' on the draft, the buyer is formally obligated to pay within the stated time.

Credit cards

Many U.S. exporters of other products (low dollar value) that are sold directly to the end user accept Visa and MasterCard in payment for export sales.

Open account

In a foreign transaction, an open account is a convenient method of payment and may be satisfactory if the buyer is well established, has demonstrated a long and favorable payment record, or has been thoroughly checked for creditworthiness. Under an open account, the exporter simply bills the customer, who is expected to pay under the agreed terms at a future date. Some of the largest firms abroad make purchases only on an open account.

Open account sales do pose risks. In the event of a non-payment, the exporter may have to pursue collection abroad, which can be difficult and costly. Before issuing a pro forma invoice to a buyer, exporters contemplating a sale on open account terms should thoroughly examine the political, economic, and commercial risks, and consult with their bankers if financing will be needed for the transaction.

Other Payment Methods

Consignment

In international consignment sales, the material is shipped to a foreign distributor to be sold on behalf of the exporter. The exporter retains title to the goods until they are sold by the distributor. Once the goods are sold, payment is sent to the exporter and any unsold products are sent to the exporter. This method poses risk to the exporter and may have to wait quite a while to get paid.

When this type of sale is made, it may be wise to consider some form of risk insurance. In addition, it may be necessary to conduct a credit check on the foreign distributor.

Counter-trade and barter

Simple barter is direct exchange of goods or services between two parties' without money changes hands. Exporters should bear in mind that counter trade often involves higher transaction costs and greater risks than simple export transactions.

Foreign currency

One of the uncertainties of foreign trade is the unpredictability of the future exchange rates between currencies. The relative value between the dollar and the buyer's currency may change between the time the deal is made and the time payment is received. Consult your banker on how to mitigate risk of currency fluctuations and what would be the acceptable payment medium, dollar versus foreign currency at the time of payment.

Determining Methods of Payment

Before you determine customers' payment methods, you need to take into consideration which would be the best option, given your circumstances and priorities and also factor in customer's willingness to accept your terms.
Other variables that have direct impact on methods of payment are:

- Your cash flow needs. If you are operating on a shoe string budget it is best you do business either payment in advance or letters of credit.
- Relationship of customer. You can always give terms to your trustworthy customers who have proved themselves in paying their bills on time.

- Economic conditions of foreign country. One of Southern California exporter who has substantial business in Asian countries, China, South Korea and Japan had been informed of Asian crisis and potential restriction of foreign currency long before it happed in late 1990's. Based on the information he received, requested each of his customers to pay in advance before financial turmoil occurred. He survived very well while his U.S. competitors doing business in Asia suffered financial setbacks and cash squeeze during the crisis.
- Type of product. If you have a premium or unique line, you can always ask customer to pay in advance or do business with the next best option, letters of credit.
- Terms of competitors are offering. If your competitors are offering terms, you need to be competitive to stay in the global game by matching their payment methods.

Documentation, shipping and logistics

When preparing to ship a product overseas, the exporter needs to be aware of packing, labeling, documentation, and insurance requirements. Because the goods are being shipped by unknown carriers to customers abroad, the new exporter must be sure that all shipping requirements are met. The traffic or export manager must make sure that the merchandise is:

- Packed correctly so that it arrives in good condition.
- Labeled correctly to ensure that the goods are handled properly and arrive on time and at the right place.
- Documented correctly to meet U.S. and foreign government requirements as well as proper collection standards.
- Insured against damage, loss, pilferage, and in some cases, delay.

Because of the considerations involved in the physical export process, most exporters, both new and experienced, rely on an international freight forwarder to perform these services.

Freight forwarders

The international freight forwarder acts as an agent for the exporter in moving cargo to the overseas destination. These agents are familiar with the import rules and regulations of foreign countries, methods of shipping, U.S. government export regulations, and the documents connected with foreign trade.

Freight forwarders can assist with an order from the start by advising the exporter of the freight costs, port charges, consular fees, cost of special documentation, and insurance costs as well as their handling fees – all of which help in preparing price quotations. Freight forwarders may also recommend the type of packing for best protecting the merchandise in transit; they can arrange to have the merchandise packed at the port or containerized. The cost for their services is the export cost that should be figured into the price charged to the customer.

When the order is ready to ship, freight forwarders should be able to review the letter of credit, commercial invoices and packing list to ensure that everything is in order. They can also reserve the necessary space on board an ocean vessel, if the exporter desires.

If the cargo arrives at the port of export before the exporter, freight forwarders may make the necessary arrangements with customs brokers to ensure that the goods comply with customs export documentation regulations. Also, they may have the goods delivered to the carrier in time for loading. They may also prepare the bill of lading and any special required documentation. After shipment, they forward all documents directly to the customer or to the paying bank if desired.

Documentation

The following documents are commonly used in exporting:

- Commercial invoice – It is a bill for the goods from the buyer to the seller.
- Bill of Lading – It is a contract between the owner of the goods and the carrier.
- Consular invoice – Certain nations require a consular invoice, which is used to control and identify goods.

- Certificate of origin – Certain nations require a signed statement as to the origin of the export item. Such certificates are obtained through the local chamber of commerce.
- Inspection certification – Some purchasers and countries may require a certificate of inspection that documents the specifications of the shipped goods.
- Dock receipt and warehouse receipt.
- Destination control statement – This statement appears on the commercial invoice, ocean or air waybill of lading.
- Insurance certificate.
- Shipper's export declaration – It is prepared and submitted to the customs agent for shipment by mail valued at more than $500 and for shipments other than mail valued at more than $2500.
- Export license.
- Export packing list – It lists the material in each individual package and indicates the type of package: box, crate, drum or carton.

Documentation must be precise. Slight discrepancies or omissions may prevent U.S. merchandise from being exported, resulting in U.S. firms not getting paid, or even leading to a seizure of the exporter's goods by U.S. or foreign government customs.

Intellectual Property Rights

Intellectual property rights are one of the complicated areas of international trade. In this high-tech era, CD's, computer games, video and innovative products and software are duplicated at the speed of light. Sometimes counterfeits are on the market within hours and generating more sales and profits than the actual product marketing and sales, while the original product owner cannot do anything about it.

This problem is complex. However, there is a great deal of enforced legal protection for intellectual property in industrialized countries, such as in the U.S. In emerging markets, there is not a history of legal protection for intellectual property, and little, if any, enforcement.

Before you start exporting, you can check with the U.S. Foreign Commercial Service to determine the patent protection laws of the particular country to which you want to sell. But be forewarned, in some instances there would be no legal restrictions to someone knocking off your product soon after it is released. You should immediately register your trademark in the country to which you intend to export. In the U.S. trademarks are issued on a "first person to use the name" basis, while in most foreign countries trademarks are issued on the basis of "first person to register".

In addition to registering your patent in the countries to which you will export, you may be able to protect your exclusivity by entering into a licensing agreement with a local manufacturer. That way you can collect royalties on your patented technology, while at the same time manufacture abroad. It becomes a win-win situation.

Piracy can be contained by making your products or services affordable in the target market. For example Microsoft made low-priced Windows XP Starter Edition for China, India, Brazil, and other emerging markets and avoided piracy considerably.

Generally speaking, fighting foreign patent infringement is not worth the cost. If you try to protect yourself from foreign patent infringement in every market, it could be a very costly and there is no guarantee that you will succeed.

Global Readiness Guide
in a Shrinking World

Managing Cultural Differences

When conducting business with our counterparts, we are constantly affected by global issues and cultural differences. Knowledge about different cultures helps us to understand what makes people unique in terms of their customs, traditions, values and beliefs; different countries and nationalities have diverse attitudes and concepts, hierarchies and roles, time and space relations and both verbal and nonverbal communication processes. The important step to developing cultural awareness is to understand the main characteristics of our own culture. For example, American businesspeople are impatient to get down to business relationships. However, in Middle Eastern and Asian countries, people invest considerable amounts of time in friendly conversation and friendships before going into their business agenda.

Believing that people think the same way around the world is a problem and a barrier to emotionally connecting with people. A good example is Stephen Covey's book, "Seven Habits of Highly Effective People." It was first published in Japan, and sold less than 5,000 copies. Given that it was a number one best seller in the U.S., many observers were surprised. In his analysis of the problem, Covey's associate pinpointed that it was because of the specific translation of the book. A virtually direct translation of the book had been made from English to Japanese, due to the belief that what worked in the U.S. would work just as well in Japan. After the discovery that this did not work, a new culturally-aware translation was then commissioned. Instead of a literal translation from English, the book was re-worded to convey meaning in a style that fit the Japanese way of thinking. This new version sold over 500,000 copies, and for a period was the number one best selling book in Japan.

Cultural competency covers three elements:

- Cultural awareness. This involves understanding one's culture and how it impacts the thinking and attitude of the people.
- Cultural sensitivity. This is the ability to respect cultural differences.
- Developing the right attitude to respond to different situations.

We need to see both the differences and similarities in each culture. When your company tries to establish a global presence, you should travel to the target country to experience first-hand your customers' consumption patterns and the habits of your products. Eventually, the data you collect will help you decide which products need to be changed slightly, totally reinvented, or require subtle adaptation to fit into the local culture.

The cultural gap can be minimized through variety ways:
- Localizing a product/service.
- Changing the product.
- Repositioning the product.
- Expanding product applications.
- Extending a local face.
- Thinking globally and acting locally

Localizing a product and or a service:

Any company that is interested in marketing internationally needs to partake in well thought-out research to eliminate future problems. For example, Nokia introduced wireless phones with a dust-resistant keypad and built-in flashlight for truck drivers who travel on India's poorly lit roads.

Changing the product:

It may be necessary for companies to change their entire product to make it appealing to their foreign consumers. For example, Kraft remade their popular Oreo cookies to look like wafers in China when the executives of the company saw that the cookie-wafer segment was growing faster than traditional biscuit-like cookies. The new Chinese Oreo consisted of four layers of crispy wafer filled with vanilla and chocolate cream, coated in chocolate. Kraft's efforts well paid off in doubling its Oreo sales in China.

Repositioning the product

Any repositioning effort in the product goes a long way. For example, it is difficult to sell diet drinks in Japan, because people are not overweight by Western standards - except Sumo wrestlers - and the word "diet" connotes a very unpleasant concept. Coke changed the name of the drink to Coke Light and focused on "figure maintenance" as opposed to "weight loss" in their promotional material. This positioning switch made the product acceptable to those Japanese women who watch their diet, yet do not like to admit that they are dieting.

Expanding product applications

Business owners' research and observation on foreign consumers' product applications can also help them to take advantage of hidden market opportunities to increase sales and profits. For example, Turbo Tek Inc., which invented a hose attachment for washing cars, has found that foreign customers are expanding the product's functions: In Japan, Turbo-Wash is used for cleaning bamboo, while the Dutch used it to wash windows and plants.

Extending Local Face

Hiring local professional people can contribute to higher success levels of when you are doing business abroad. You need distribution agents in foreign   locations who can handle negotiation, speak the local language and has the ability to find customers. For example, UPS hires local managers and values their services in the countries they do business. As CEO Mike Eskew stated, "Our business runs best when we empower local people and make a commitment to them."

Thinking Globally and Acting Locally

Once you understand cultural differences, you are prepared to "think globally and act locally" which gives you an edge to create commercial opportunities in the target country. The McDonald food chain is a perfect example of thinking and acting locally. In all their overseas markets, they tailor their product offerings to meet local preferences. In Japan, they sell noodles as well as burgers. In Germany, they have beer on the menu. In vegetarian India they sell soy burgers. The company has created unique local revenue streams in foreign countries in addition to their core product, "Big Macs".

How to Learn Culture

You can get information by reading publications of major Accounting firms that have subsidiaries based in that country, or put it a request at the State Department' with an official who handles the specific country's desk.

Communicating with people through the Internet and the phone can be a great source for learning certain characteristics of that particular culture.

Going International by Lewis Griggs and Lennie Copeland, Do's, *Taboos* by Roger Axtell and the Department of Commerce's *Publication on International Business Practices* are all excellent reads to learn more about the different aspects of every culture.

Global Knowledge is Power

Technology has not only intensified the local and global competition, it has also empowered the customer to become extremely savvy in terms of product, brand and information choices. It has become critical to hire managers who are knowledgeable with respect to different cultures, customers, suppliers and distribution channels so that they can work across borders with ease. There are ample resources, such as books, CD-ROMs, universities, special courses, and events organized by international trade associations to master skills required to succeed internationally.

Global managers need to strike a balance between their visions of embracing the culture of binding everyone together within the organization and the process of respecting and encouraging local and market-sensitive cultures to achieve long-term success.

For example, when the U.S. company Frito-Lay wanted to establish a European presence, it acquired snack food companies in European countries, such as Spain, Portugal and Uzay Gida in Turkey. The company took many instrumental steps towards building Frito-Lay Europe by respecting local cultures with varied tastes and preferences. Bill McLaughlin, the CEO of Frito Lay, came up with an effective strategy:

- Develop a strong team based on celebrating differences.
- Create the best set of values to build trust and understanding.
- Identify specific cultural preferences pertaining to the flavors of snacks.

- Shift from a variety of different brands to one with local presence by printing the Frito-Lay "sun and banner" logo on the packages.
- Put together quality standards that are aimed at manufacturing premium products.
- Build or buy a powerful brand that has sterling local reputation.
- Focus on a central theme and symbol to bind together the business system, brand and consumers.

Culturally-competent managers look beyond their boundaries to seek innovative ideas for new products and services. A competent innovator can try new methods, find new associations to create his/her own brands, and search for unique opportunities to generate something greater than a sum of the parts. When the Beatles went to India, they fell in love with the mystical Eastern music while they were there, and the music they created with their Indian partner was a delightful combination of East and West.

Global Openness

Global managers have an awareness and appreciation of diversity across cultures and markets and see it as a valuable tool to compete in the global marketplace.

Managers need to ask themselves several questions to see whether they have the necessary global mindset and ready to take on the world:

- Are you open to ideas regardless of where they are coming from?

- How comfortable are you with new cultural experiences?
- Do Your Company's Team Members Have a Global Mindset?
- Is your organization willing to pursue global opportunities to diversify its sales and profits?
- Do your team members perceive value in expanding into the world marketplace to bring in a healthy dose of novelty and creativity into their company?

Culture

Culture determines who we are, and how we think and react. It also includes our beliefs and values. The United States is a diverse country in terms of different cultures. America is a country of immigrants, and the culture in the East coast is entirely different than the South. This gives Americans ample chances to see differences firsthand and get prepared to take the competition to a global scale.

We need to assess who we are and how we come across to others to be able to understand and differentiate other cultures. American business people can be described as being entrepreneurial, result-oriented and have a tendency to attach importance on time. They believe in the saying, "time is money." Americans are friendly and display informality, preferring to be on a first-name basis with their business counterparts. This shortens the time to get to know each other and feel comfortable with others.

How cultures differ:

- Space – Americans are fond of their space, especially preferring distance when they are talking to people. On the other hand, Latin and Eastern cultures want to come close when they are communicating.
- Dress and Appearance – National garments can be both formal and informal. Become familiar with a country's "dress code" and when in doubt, dress conservatively. You can always take off your jacket or tie off.
- Punctuality – Germans are very prompt while Latinos have a more relaxed attitude towards time.
- Relationships – In Turkish culture, people have a great deal of respect for elders and teachers.
- Values – Material values matter in determining the success level of individuals in the United States. In some Pacific Island cultures, as people acquire more wealth, they are expected to give away more or share with others.
- Workplace attitudes and values – Countries like Belgium, Brazil, Chile and Mexico came high on the score of accepting unequal distribution of power in institutions and organizations, according to a study by Dr. Pearce of Claremont School.
- Societies being individualistic or collectivist- The former are noted for people who are self-reliant and value independence and achievement. Ranking high on this measure were Argentina, Germany, Britain and Norway. People in countries with a collectivism orientation tend to gravitate towards groups, such as relatives, teams and organizations, and expect the group to take care of them in

exchange for absolute loyalty. High scorers include Greece, Indonesia, Spain and Thailand. (Wall Street Journal, July 7, 2008, "Follow the Leaders", Dr. Pearce, Professor of Management at Claremont School).

- Source and expression of identity – An individual's likely identification with self or group. Japanese people are group oriented.
- Entertaining – In many cultures, being entertaining sets the stage to build relationships. Find out where the entertainment will take place. If it is a private home, gifts (flowers, wine) are appropriate to the host or hostess. When in doubt always ask locals to get answers. Even the Concierge at your hotel can be a good source to figure out what gifts to present your foreign host/hostess with.
- Gift giving – Your research on what to give as a gift to your counterpart goes a long way. For example, the worst gift that you can give to your Chinese counterpart would be a clock, which Chinese people associate with death and termination of relationships.
- Topics considered appropriate for discussion – In China and Turkey, people feel comfortable discussing their salaries and marital status, which would be seen as inappropriate by Americans.
- Eye contact – Direct eye contact is critical in U.S. culture and associated with respect and honesty. In Asian and Latin American cultures, avoiding direct eye contact shows respect. In India, eye contact is associated with social status and people from different social background do not make eye contact.

- Business cards – If you are visiting Asian countries, have a large supply of cards with you. When you receive a business card from your business partner, hold it with two hands and take time to read it. It shows your respect to him/her.

High-Context and Low-Context Cultures

Indirect communication is the high-context culture and you need to be familiar with social, political and personal context to be able to understand the whole message. The responsibility to understand is on the receiver. This type of communication is prevalent in Eastern cultures. While in low-context cultures, such as the United States and Australia, people mean what they say in their straight-forward way of communicating with others. And there is no room for misinterpretation of messages.

Stereotyping Blocks Communication

Stereotyping is a way of assigning attributes to people who belong to a certain group. Often these attributes are the result of some preconceptions or prejudgment, For example, seeing all the Islamic fundamentalists as terrorists is a stereotype. We need to get rid of stereotypes and judge people on their merits to build strong relationships with our business counterparts.

Culturally Sensitive Marketing

Global managers must develop an interest to learn and do their research diligently to be able to see both the differences and similarities of cultures. Inquisitiveness, research and observation are the key factors behind global managerial success for coming up with the right product and services aimed at a target market.

Managers need to travel frequently to meet and get to know their counterparts, customers and employees to have a solid understanding of their end-users needs and expectations. A great example is the former CEO of Procter and Gamble, John Pepper, who made a habit of reaching out to five of his customers by visiting them in their homes. He wanted to talk with the families and ask pertinent questions on the usage of his company's products. His actions clearly indicated the fact that international travel is critical to learn more about various countries, local cultures, and consumers that make up a major portion of the company's global business. His travels also confirmed the belief that French people prefer the front-load washers to top-load washers. This particular information helped him accept the duality of managing a new cold-water detergent brand on a global basis, while at the same time finding a way to meet the local needs of getting the detergent to distribute evenly during the wash process when used in front-load washers. Eventually the company came up with a new product based on a plastic ball, which was filled with detergent and placed in the front-load washer along with the dirty clothes.

When a company tries to establish a global presence, its executives need to travel to the target country to see first-hand their foreign consumer's consumption patterns and habits of their products. The data they acquire will help them decide either to adapt their products to the local culture or to come up with entirely new products.

Product Design

Design is an integral part of marketing efforts to come up with products that are universal, functional, user friendly and aesthetically pleasing for end users in foreign countries.

A Guideline of Global Product Design

Factor: Change	Potential Product
High technology content	Product simplification
High labor content labor	Automation: Low cost
Level of income	Quality and price change
Climate differences	Product adaptation
Special conditions	Product redesign or reinvention

Foreign Language Proficiency

Although English is widely spoken around the world, many professionals, government officials, consumers and end-users speak it as second language and are not knowledgeable on American English nuances, slang and idioms, which block the communication process among businesspeople. American executives who cannot speak a foreign language must rely on translators and interpreters.

Some tips when hiring a translator:

- Translators should be accredited by the American Translators Association in both the required language and knowledge of the subject matter. For example, Spanish and medical terminology.

- Translators should understand the actual and intended meaning and knowledgeable on that particular industry and technical jargon.

There are many options for businesspeople to do their own research on the internet to find out some companies which offer crash courses on languages.

Some Cultural Resources

- American Graduate School of International Management, Thunderbird, Glendale, Arizona
- American Management Associations, New York, NY
- American Society for Training and Development, Alexandria, VA
- Berlitz Schools of Language of America, Princeton , NJ
- U.S. State Department, Country Desk

International Sales Process

International marketing is not different from local marketing when it comes to establishing trust and confidence with your foreign associates. Your first contact with a potential foreign customer will most likely be by letter, phone, fax or e-mail.

Some effective communication tips are:

- State clearly your needs.

- Understand customer needs.
- What can your company deliver based on the needs of your customers?
- What is established sales patterns in a foreign country?

International business is definitely a long term investment in building relationships with your foreign partners. Learning their language and knowing the country, culture and your foreign buyer consists of the entire package of nurturing ties with them. As Turkish businessman said: "To really get access and establish in Turkish market, have raki (strong Turkish hard liquor) at long dinners with them"; and enjoy the social exchange and engage in philosophical conversations with your Turkish business associates. And one tip of advice and caution about raki, exercise prudence when drinking it, because it is by no means light liquor, and definitely does not stay like it is in the bottle.

Global selling tips:

- Be ready and do your homework. Read books on social and business etiquette, history and cultural values.
- Speak at least a couple of words in their language to impress your host/hostess.
- Respect their culture.
- Do not sign any contracts unless you have them reviewed by an attorney who is well versed in the legal system of your target country.
- Register your trademark. The intellectual property laws are not fully enforced in some countries.

- Patience is a virtue. Once you offer your proposal, don't expect to get a quick response.
- When you advertise, take into account the cultural factors to avoid making major blunders.

Some well known international mistakes:

- General Motors thought its Nova car could be marketed in Latin America. Later they found out that "Nova" in Spanish means "it does not go."
- Gerber had a picture of a baby on its labels. The product did not do well in some part of Africa where there was a high level of illiteracy; the parents thought that the food was for white babies only.
- Kentucky Fried Chicken's "finger licking good" became "eat your fingers off" in the Chinese translation.
- The Dairy Association's "Got Milk" campaign was advertised in Mexico and translation said: "Are you lactating?"

Styles of Presentation

Cultural factors play an important role in your presentation styles to make the most impact on your foreign partners. Some cultures prefer formal presentations that include hard data including facts, figures and graphs. Others focus on the emotional connection that they can build with their audience. Some universal tips on presentations are:

- Active participation. People love to be included and participated in the material that you are presenting to your audience. Invite them to share their ideas, comments and suggestions which will give them a huge sense of empowerment and eventually help you to bond with your audience.
- Imagery and metaphors. You can present your material with universally acceptable imagery and metaphors which will help them to see the big picture. For example, if you say in your presentation that we need to manufacture or build more BMWs here as opposed to Volkswagons, people can visualize better with the images associated with these cars and buyer characteristics, which will eventually eliminate the cross cultural barriers and get the attention of your participants.

New Global Thinking

We need to be effective global change agents to be able to survive in a borderless world. The old way of thinking and confining our thoughts, imagination and most importantly our businesses to national borders would definitely defeat us in the long term.

The key is adopting the global outlook and making the kind of changes both in our lives and the organizations in which we work; and we can achieve the much needed global mindset by:

- "Seeing the world as a whole." Being comfortable with the flow of capital, ideas, people and ideas, and determining where we fit in within the global picture.

- "Willing to Contribute." See cultural differences as an advantage rather than challenges that we need to cope with, and adopt the attitude to share our strengths with others to start building meaningful relationships.

- "Ready to compromise." Global exchange is a two way street. Everyone involved in relationships needs to do their share to achieve long term partnerships.

We need to lead the change with a global edge, and be extraordinarily equipped with the knowledge and skills aimed at empowering us to make a difference in the world.

The Art of Cross-Cultural Negotiation

Negotiation is the process of communicating back and forth between two or more parties for the purpose of reaching a joint agreement on different needs or ideas. In the art of negotiation, persuasion, rather than power, is used.

We can negotiate price, terms, delivery, quality service, training and resources. The same basic rules apply to global negotiation, except we have to factor in the cultural factors, which make it both challenging and exciting for both parties. We need to focus on interests, not positions, and meet the needs of the other side and respond to the question of, "What's in it for them?"

The stages of negotiation

- Orientation and fact-finding. Orientation involves learning about the organizations of the other side, understanding the cultural factors and individual style of your counterparts, and knowing the history of similar negotiations.

- Resistance. If there is no resistance there will not be genuine interest on part of your counterpart. The most common strategy in negotiation is people resisting the price.

- Reformulation of strategies. As you gather new data you will need to asses entirely new situations.

- Hard bargaining and decision making. This is the time to create options that will be mutually agreeable for both parties.

- Agreement.

- Follow up.

Global negotiation requires identifying and prioritizing the issues and seeing them through cultural lenses and finally arriving at win-win solutions in achieving long-term relations with our foreign counterparts.

Strength of Persuasion

Aristotle defined persuasion by ethos (credibility), logos (logic) and pathos (emotion), and he stressed that three ingredients need to be there for people to persuade others. In negotiation, credibility means the person has the status and knowledge base; logic implies having facts and figures at his/her disposal; finally, pathos means having the power to connect with people on an emotional level to persuade other individuals.

Ethos (credibility) means a lot for Eastern cultures, as they are extremely rank-conscious. If you, as an American, are selecting a team of negotiators, you need to pay attention to the status and positions of Middle-Easterners. Arab culture places importance to high education standards, having degree from a top American school and a good family background. However, majority of Americans value most to what you have accomplished in life that involves work and life experiences.

Americans aim for closing the deal within the shortest amount of time; the same deal may take their counterparts much longer. Americans need to be patient during the negotiation process. Losing temper or making an angry remark of an American partner has the potential to end a negotiation process immediately. Japanese see persuasion as a compromise in setting the stage of closing the deal. Several factors are critical during the persuasion stage when you are negotiating with Japanese. Among those are: keeping the negotiation momentum with harmony, and securing the agreement of all of the participants.

Negotiation starts with trust

Before starting the negotiation process with our partners, we need to have some type of informal meeting to get to know each other and see the issues, interests and concerns in a relaxed atmosphere. This gives us the opportunity to look at the big picture and gain more time to prioritize our interests and how we can achieve an agreement that will be satisfactory for both sides.

Even though trust is a universal concept and most societies see it as an ingredient of a strong relationship, the interpretation and definition of trust varies from culture to culture. Americans perceive it as a responsibility of their actions. For the Malaysians, trust means strong loyalty and commitment.

Global businesspeople are culture-builders; they listen and share what they learn from around the world about building strong bonds through long-term alliances and connections to minimize the differences. Adopting a global mindset and determination are critical in collaborating cross-culturally to focus on similarities and see differences as a learning experience along the way. Japanese value group decisions and harmony in negotiations, while Arabs put emphasis on personal relationships.

Guidelines for Effective Cross Cultural Negotiation

A competent international negotiator is well-prepared and aware of cultural differences to be able to demonstrate maximum effectiveness in the negotiation process. Here are some valuable tips for improving those skills:

- Study other cultures– Learn about the country, culture and counterpart's social and business background ahead of time. Knowledge will give you the necessary ammunition on what to observe and how to conduct effective negotiation. Also attending pre-negotiation social activities will prepare you better for the main task.

- Know yourself - Americans are independent to tackle any challenge that comes their way during negotiation and don't like to beat around the bush; they are impatient to get to the heart of the matter. They also favor the "deal is deal" approach and give a hundred percent when it comes to honoring the agreement.

- Power of silence – Don't underestimate the power of silence; it gives you a huge break to gather your thoughts and to think about your next move. Your silence also gives your counterpart to take the first initiative, which in essence shifts the power to you as well.

- Give and take - The centerpiece of any American negotiation is based on give-and-take. This particular approach is not applicable in many foreign cultures, so instead of getting frustrated, you need to find out in advance their way and style of negotiation.

- Work out differences – Misunderstanding happens all the time. The best way to deal with it is to paraphrase what is being said, and get clarification from the other side to get to the bottom of the issue, and then try to clear the air and move on.

- Binding contract versus non-binding contract – America is a litigious society, and businessmen feel comfortable if they have a binding contract to avoid potential problems later. However, in Asian countries such as Korea, China and Japan, people value relationships more than strict contracts. You need to handle this issue in the most diplomatic way without hurting the feelings of your counterparts.

- Selection of Negotiators- American negotiators are selected on the basis of their technical knowledge and experience on the issues being negotiated. However, their counterparts may have status and power in the hierarchy, but lack competence to comprehend what is being discussed. Also, people in Mexico select their team members on the basis of excellent presentation skills and a good command of the language.

- Smoothing differences by a middle man – Japanese business people do not express their disagreements directly during negotiation. Instead, they prefer to seek the services of middle men who serve as the peace-maker, so that the negotiation process continues uninterrupted.

- Contingency plan – Prior to negotiation, some negotiators devise different alternatives they can fall back on when negotiation goes through a stage of stalemate. Other cultures stick to only one position that they originally favor, and prevent the other party from discussing other options.

- Women negotiators – In most cultures, women are not taken seriously and not perceived as tough negotiators. To overcome this particular and unfair common perception, it is best to select a female who has the best credentials and knowledge to head the team. Hilal Baskal, one of my close friends and classmates from college, was assigned as the first woman Turkish Ambassador to an Arab country, Bahrain. During her tenure as the highest ranking government official, she also negotiated a series of agreements between Turkey and Bahrain. She says: "Being first and woman is always an advantage. I had the most pleasant experience in terms of being treated with respect and was instrumental in getting to the fruition of a series of negotiations." Based on several studies, women have amazing strength in reading people through non-verbal communication, as well as a strong intuition that helps them pick up some important messages in assessing their counterpart's position. The fact that women are consensus builders and respect other people's opinions makes them strong candidates to be excellent negotiators. Having patience and favoring long-term gratification are also great assets for women since international relations are built over time.

- Using Services of Interpreter- Selection of a competent interpreter is important when negotiators face language barriers. Their experience in the language and knowledge are critical in the selection process. The interpreter that was assigned to me during the CAFTA (Central America Free Trade Agreement) Meeting in 2005 in Guatemala barely spoke English, which made my job extremely difficult. Make sure to avoid such unpleasant surprises in your overseas visits by asking about the competency level of your translators.

- Never discuss your departure time with others- You need to use discretion and tactfulness when handling your foreign counterpart's favorite question: "When are you leaving?" If you give an accurate question you may face the risk of being pressured to an undesirable deal that would not be acceptable on your part. Otherwise, your answer would probably be: "I am having fabulous time and enjoying my stay in your great country and have not decided my departure date yet."

- Understand politeness- American culture is very much defined by its pragmatic and bottom-line characteristics, in which people open up easily and speak their mind in the most expressive ways. Some Eastern cultures put so much emphasis on titles based on nobility and formality, that it takes considerable time on their part to start a direct negotiation process.

In the world of intensified trade and globalization, sharpening our skills in stating your BATNA (Best Alternative to Negotiating Agreement), framing the issues properly and most importantly, being aware of the cultural implications are crucial to arrive at mutually satisfactory negotiation with our foreign partners.

Top Four Countries (Canada, Mexico, Japan and China) for U.S. Exports

How Canada, Mexico, Japan and China differ culturally from the U.S.

Canada

Nafta (North Atlantic Free Trade Agreement) was signed between the United States and Canada in 1988 to reduce trade barriers and intensify trade between the two countries. The agreement resulted in creating a series of joint ventures, acquisitions and branch offices in each country. The relationship between the U.S. and Canada is the closest and most extensive in the world. It is reflected in bilateral trade – the equivalent of $1.5 billion a day in goods, as well as in people-to-people contacts with the 300,000 people who cross the shared border every day. In 2007, total trade between the two countries exceeded $560 billion.

Canada's importance to the U.S. is not just on a border-state level: Canada is the leading export market for 36 U.S. states, and is ranked in the top three for another 10 states. Canada has a predominantly service-based economy with a large manufacturing base. The U.S. is Canada's largest foreign investor, and constitutes 59% of all foreign investment.

Canada is a multi-cultural country (French and English), and Canadians value their distinct identity separate from the U.S. and do not want to be perceived as an extension of the U.S. in terms of culture. Canada, being in close proximity to the U.S. and an English-speaking country, is attractive to export-minded American business people to do business with.

Here are some tips that Americans can use when doing business with their neighbors:

- Canadian negotiators are selected on the basis of experience, knowledge and loyalty to their organizations, and they are expected to set aside their personal agendas during the negotiation process.

- Always take into account of a negotiator's heritage; English Canadians favor a direct communication style, and their words reflect their intent. However, the French rely only partially on words, and non-verbal communication dominates the communication process.

- Canadians prefer to be treated as equals and with respect by their American counterparts, and any comparisons of American and Canadian culture do not go over well with them.

- Canadians come to negotiation well-prepared and prefer to tackle the issues and challenges one at a time. Americans have a direct approach of "take it or leave it" which can backfire and result in irreparable damage when arriving at an agreement.

- Be aware of the term "split the difference" which means that the buyer will end up paying more.

- Make sure you use dual language, by having both English and French on your product labels and packaging, which will allow you to target both English and French speaking territories in Canada.

- Trust is an important ingredient of any negotiation for Canadians, and they expect that their counterparts will adhere to achieving mutual goals in the negotiation process.

- French Canadians value the protocol side of the business, so make sure that you pay attention to the details of the ceremonial aspect of the negotiation.

- Appropriate gifts that you can give to Canadians are inexpensive items, such as flowers.

Mexico

Mexico is the most populous Spanish-speaking country in the world, and the second most-populous country in Latin America, after Portuguese-speaking Brazil.

Mexico is highly dependent on exports to the U.S. which represent more than quarter of the country's GDP. Mexico's trade regime is among the most open in the world with free trade agreements with the US, Canada and the European Union.

Mexico, in its efforts to revitalize its economy and open up to international competition, sought closer relations with the U.S, Western Europe and the Pacific Basin.

U.S. relations with Mexico are as important and complex as with any country in the world. U.S. relations with Mexico have a direct impact on the lives and livelihoods of millions of Americans – whether the issue is trade or economic reform. The U.S. and Mexico are partners in Nafta, and enjoy broad and expanding trade relations. Nafta helped Mexico privatize state-owned enterprises and opened up the country to massive foreign direct investments. The trade agreement also covers intellectual property and environment.

Mexicans have conflicting attitudes towards Americans. They admire their powerful neighbor and the perfect quality of American products, but at the same time harbor suspicion and cannot get over the historical pain of the U.S. annexation of Southwest. Mexicans made substantial economic progress over the years, and it would be nice on the part of Americans to give credit for their achievements, which will help Americans start negotiations on a positive note.

Here are some tips in Understanding the Mexican culture:

- Family – Family and friends matter most to Mexicans. They have a tendency to do business with people they intimately know.

- People are preferred to be addressed by "Senor" (for man) and "Senora" (for women).

- Good conversation subjects are: Mexican culture, art, history and the country's natural scenery.

- Value of speaking Spanish– Speaking a few Spanish words can help to build rapport with your counterpart.

- Don't be surprised when the meetings do not start on time. They refer to American promptness as "Hora Americana," something you rarely experience in Mexico.

- Mexicans are not in favor of structured meetings and do not rush negotiations. In the event of a cancelled meeting, they go with the flow instead of getting upset about it.

- Mexicans prefer diplomacy and tactfulness over a confrontational style. If anything goes wrong during the negotiation, they shy away from addressing the issue head-on.

- Hierarchical nature of their business gives the authority of decision-making to the person who has the ultimate power. That particular person can be head of the family or the person in the higher echelon of the organization.

- Mexico is a formal society, and formality is also reflected in their professional appearance of business people.

- Mexico is not a change-oriented culture and people prefer status quo over change.

- Establishing harmony is always preferred to disagreements and disputes.

- Mexicans use non-verbal communication including hand gestures and other emotional signs when they are trying to convey their message to others.

- They are risk-averse, subject to resignation and fatalistic.

- They love to bargain. Always have room for leverage in bargaining by setting your original price high.

- "Manana" (Tomorrow) is a term you will hear often in Mexico and has two different meanings for Mexicans. One meaning being: things can be deferred to a later time; another meaning is as the Americans understand: "Tomorrow is another day" which implies hope and a positive attitude.

China

China's entry into the World Trade Organization in 2001 was a major milestone for Chinese economy in terms of expansion of business and international trade. China represents a vast market that has yet to be fully tapped and a low-cost base for export-oriented production. China is forging ahead educational partnerships with exchanges with foreign universities which have helped to create research opportunities for its students.

China's ongoing economic transformation has had a profound impact not only on China but on the entire world. The market-oriented reforms China has implemented over the past two decades have unleashed individual initiative and entrepreneurship. The result has been the largest reduction of poverty and one of the fastest increases in income levels ever seen. Today, China has the fourth-largest economy in the world.

As part of China's integration into the World Trade Organization, tariffs were lowered and market impediments abolished, which opened new markets for U.S. providers of service like banking, insurance and telecommunications. China has made significant progress implementing its WTO commitments, but serious concerns remain in the area of intellectual property rights protection.

U.S. direct investments in China cover a wide range of manufacturing sectors, several large hotel projects and restaurant chains. U.S. companies entered into a series of joint ventures, wholly foreign-owned enterprises in China. Total two-way trade between China and the United States grew from $33 billion in 1992 to over $386 billion in 2007.

Some negotiation tips for American business people:

- Negotiation with Chinese takes a long time because decisions are made collectively and the red tape is still a norm in the system.

- Preparation and letting your Chinese counterparts know what you will undertake there ahead of time is essential for both parties. It will help you twofold: you will be ready when the Chinese raise questions regarding your proposal and you will also avoid last minute surprises which may otherwise put both parties in difficult situations.

- Hard bargaining is entrenched in their culture; you are expected to make concessions during the negotiation. Instead of focusing on price, make your concessions on minor aspects of the agreement such as delivery, service and warranties.

- You have to work hard to earn their trust in the beginning. Once you establish trust, you gain a long-term loyal friend.

- Two Chinese magic words help you to open doors of communication with your business partners: "Doe-jay" (Thank you) and "Ni hao?" (How are you?)

- If things don't go the way you planned, avoid making angry remarks, which can damage future relations with your Chinese partners.

- Americans value talent to get ahead in business; Chinese see persistence and perseverance as keys to succeed in the business world.

- There is a fundamental difference in the education system of China and the U.S. Children in the United States are taught to see things in detail and in China the same things are perceived as a whole. This very culture is reflected in negotiation styles of both countries. Chinese bundle all the details together, such as cost and delivery, during the negotiation, whereas Americans prefer to discuss each issue separately.

- China is perceived by American business people as a large market. You have to be ready to deal with separate state officials and bureaucracies of each region to generate large volume of sales, and it certainly takes a long time to capture the whole market.

- Group culture in China is prevalent, and singling out any team member of Chinese delegation is seen as a breach of etiquette.

- Sometimes the negotiation process takes longer and you need to make a couple of trips to finalize your agreement. Therefore, never burn your bridges with your Chinese business partners and always keep your eyes on the ball.

- Building your expertise and knowledge in China can give you a tremendous edge in terms of credibility and help you get cooperation from your Chinese partners.

- Negotiation is not a one shot deal in China, and you need to cultivate long-term relationships with the Chinese to get a good return on your investments (money, time and effort) there.

Japan

Japan, a country of islands, extends along the Eastern or Pacific coast of Asia. Japan is slightly smaller than California.

Japan's industrialized, free market economy is the second-largest in the world, and it represents a major economic power in Asia and around the globe. Japan's economy is highly efficient and competitive in areas linked to international trade, but productivity is far lower in areas such as agriculture, distribution and services. After achieving one of the highest economic growth rates in the world from the 1960's through the 1980's, the Japanese economy slowed dramatically in the early 1990's, when the "bubble economy" collapsed, marked by plummeting stock and real estate prices. Japan's long term economic prospects are considered good, and it has largely recovered from its worst period of economic stagnation since World War II. Japan is increasingly active in Africa and Latin America –in 2008 it concluded negotiations with Mexico and Chile on an Economic Partnership Agreement (EPA).

Because of the U.S. and Japan's combined economic and technological impact on the world, the U.S.-Japan relationship has become global in scope. The U.S. economic policy toward Japan is aimed at increasing access to Japan's markets and two-way investment; stimulating domestic demand, economic growth, and improving the climate for US investors.

Japan is a major market for many U.S. products, including chemicals, pharmaceuticals, film and music, commercial aircraft and medical and scientific supplies.

Tips on Japanese Negotiating Style:

- American business people need to achieve a long-term relationship with the Japanese.

- Unlike Americans, Japanese tend to devote more time and effort during the initial stages of the negotiation and put much emphasis on harmony.

- Japanese aim at very high prices in the initial stages of negotiation, and gradually lower the price when they see resistance from buyers. They always set room to maneuver in order to be on the safe side.

- In Japan, the decision-making process is very much characterized as a team effort and several people are involved and contribute to it.

- In Japan, you must be a good reader of body language to be able to understand what your counterpart means. Words are a very small portion of communication and you need to carefully watch body movements, tone of voice and eye contact of your counterparts. In Japan, "Hai" (Yes) is not always a positive; it may imply no as well.

- Use the word "San" after people's names, which is equivalent to Mr., Miss, Mrs. or Ms. which shows respect.

- Use simple English when you are communicating, and if you have trouble being understood, write it down. Japanese understand written English better than spoken English.

- Direct questions and abrupt comments are not welcomed by Japanese.

- If you go into a conflict situation, use the services of intermediary to smooth things out.

- Even though business women are making progress in breaking the glass ceiling in Japan, it is still a macho culture, and a majority of players and negotiators in the business world are men.

Power of Women

Global Businesswoman

In the globally interdependent world, international trade fuels economic growth for countries worldwide. U.S. exports have surged to over $1 trillion in 2008. Small firms, especially women-owned businesses, are catching up with the trend and getting involved in global trade. The studies conducted in the late 1990's, with underwriting by IBM, surveyed members of women business associations in Brazil, Canada, Ireland, Mexico and the United States and indicated the following: The firms that had revenues in excess of $500,000 is from one-third to 11 times higher among those owned by women involved in international trade than those owned by women who are involved only in their national market. This study clearly shows that exports bring in sales that translate into more profits.

The international marketplace enables successful women exporters to sharpen their competitiveness in facing the global customer base with different needs and expectations and also helps them to focus more on niche marketing and growth opportunities than firms that are not exporting overseas. Some women success stories in the international arena are:

- Candy Bouquet International, which is a franchise firm that manufactures and sells decorative candy arrangements similar to floral arrangements. Margaret McEntire founded the company in 1989 in her garage. Today, the typical Candy Bouquet store is a full-scale chocolate and candy operation, although some operates as home-based businesses. Some franchises operate exclusively as Candy Bouquet, others run this franchise under their floral shop or other retail outlet. In 2001, Candy Bouquet has over 500 franchises in 48 states and 35 other countries. Her recipe for sweet success is simple: good quality and standing one hundred percent behind her product. This has helped her establish her global business and grow internationally.

- Susan Bourma, the CEO of Capitol Hill Building Maintenance, is a self-made entrepreneur who built a successful business when there was nowhere to go but up. Bourma was born in Sierra Leone and came to the United States in 1974 to attend college. After a failed marriage she was forced to leave college and accept welfare in order to take care of her infant son. Today, she runs Capitol Hill Building Maintenance, Inc, directing cleaning services with 200 loyal staff members and generating solid profits. She participated in the Canada/USA Business Women's Trade Summit and women's trade mission to Africa in 2000 where she made a number of sales.

- Carole Sluski, President of Petrochem, and her daughter Jill, the Sales and Marketing Director, are clients of U.S. Export Assistance Center. Petrochem currently sells its oven chain lubricants in the U.S., England, South Africa, Spain and Saudi Arabia. Sluski credits the U.S. Commercial Services's Global Diversity Market Entry Program for helping her take Petrochem global.

The U.S. Commercial Service is at the service of women entrepreneurs who want to expand their businesses overseas and 160 international offices and 105 more across the U.S.

Their website is www.usatrade.gov. No matter what stage of export readiness your company is in, their network of trade specialists can provide you with the export assistance you need. The U.S. Department of Commerce will help you choose the best market for your company, design a strategy to help you get your business there and protect your interests once you have started doing business globally.

Women Involvement in International Trade

Developing women global talent, skills and leadership makes good business sense for international trade success. Women's relationship-building and communication abilities make them naturals for global business; women exporters are not just businesswomen but "social entrepreneurs" as well. Here are some ways for women to plunge into the international area:

- Service businesses - According to the latest available statistics from Small Business Administration, women-owned businesses are the fastest growing segment of all new businesses in the U.S., and more than half of these are in the service sector. Service businesses such as accounting, teaching, consulting, training, legal services provide excellent stepping-stones to go global.

- Export Business - You may own an export-oriented business and you may be on the lookout for target countries to sell your company's product/service. Either way, there is a lot of help on the part of government-owned organizations such as Small Business Development Centers, USEAC's (United States Export Assistance Centers) and in California CITD's (Center for International Trade Development) funded by Community Colleges. Their consultants and trainers can help you to put together global business plans and research your target market for you.

- Education- Certificate programs provided by well-known schools, such as UCLA Extension and US Export Assistance Centers can provide the basic training on International trade.

- Cross-cultural training –The best way to acclimate yourself in cross-cultural skills are either to take courses on the topic or to travel to that particular country to observe cultural and life styles.

- Language –Speaking the language is significant in shortening your learning curve in international training. People who speak the language have a better chance to establish rapport and build relationships. Americans who travel overseas are amazed by the local people's knowledge of variety of topics pertaining to their culture, particularly American politics and pop culture. That will help to build rapport with your partners.

- Become a member of the International Trade Family – There are wonderful organizations such as Women in International Trade and other Trade Associations, which offer a great venue for networking and getting informed about the business. If you take on some responsibilities in the groups or serve as a Member, Board Member or Director, you will be able to build your valuable database in a short time and maybe go even further to make an impact on target audiences.

The time is right for women to demonstrate their strength, and showcase their creativity and can-do attitude towards global business. Advances in travel, technology and telecommunications have leveled the playing field for even the smallest women-owned businesses to expand their sales abroad. Business growth does not have to be limited any longer by local, regional or even national borders, but can increase through the ingenuity, energy and imagination of women business owners and aspiring women international trade professionals.

Intercultural Communication Tools

Video Conferencing

Video conferencing is growing exponentially and is a great help for people in international business who would like to reduce their travel expenses, improve cross-cultural communication and extend their global reach. Anyone with a broadband Internet connection and a web browser can log onto the Internet and participate in or host a web conference, a video web conference or a webinar.

You can keep in touch with distributors, employees, business contacts and clients anywhere in the world by logging on and participating in your Internet meeting. Some video conferencing software allows more than 10 people to be seen at the same time. Participants can talk and hear one another by using standard microphones and headsets through Voice over Internet Protocol (VoIP). Participants can share applications and open and examine common documents while online. Hosts can show a PowerPoint presentation that will be visible to all attendees of the conference.

Global companies are presently using videoconferencing (internet meetings), to demonstrate their products and services to potential clients, conduct training sessions and even perform after-sales servicing of their products and software (by using remote desktop control software).

E-mail

E-mail usage is on the rise around the world. When you are e-mailing somebody, make sure your message is clear and always support it with some specific information to avoid misunderstandings. Using simple English is the best way to get your message across to your business partners.

E-mail checklist:

- Respond overseas inquiries promptly and in the language of the letter of inquiry, when requested.

- Make sure to put "U.S.A." in the address. Toll-free phone numbers in the U.S. (800,888,878) do not work abroad. Include your local telephone numbers (all 10 digits) in your e-mail.

- In your first e-mail, do not ask for credit information. Once your relationship is developed you can get this information through international banking department of your bank or the U.S. Department of Commerce.

- Present your company as a reliable supplier of your goods.

- Make sure your e-mail sets the stage to write a letter in which you provide customer with full information on your product, including price and cost to be delivered to arrival point in the buyer's country.

- Your e-mail address, telephone number and fax number is included on your e-mail.

- State the complete information in the body of the e-mail message and do not abbreviate.

Over-the-Phone Translation

Over-the-phone interpretation is mostly aimed at companies that conduct business in several languages. When you are in the country, your cell-phone gives you access to a 24-hour bilingual interpreter; once you call the service and explain what needs to be translated and hand the phone over to the person you want to speak with –for example, your foreign business partner– the message will be translated immediately. This service translates from English to over 170 languages and vice versa. Technology will enable over-the-phone interpretation companies to reduce their costs and make it affordable to a larger market of global businesspeople.

Five Pillars of Successful Global Operation

The five essential requirements to grow and expand your reach in the international marketplace are:

- Quality
- Teamwork
- Customer satisfaction
- Innovation
- Leadership

QUALITY

Quality consciousness has become an overriding consideration among U.S. suppliers and manufacturers to maintain their global competitiveness. Emphasis on quality grew rapidly among small and medium-sized companies too. They were quick to see that quality is the passport to success in both domestic and foreign markets. Small businesses need to be prepared to meet the quality challenges of international competition before they go global.

Developing global quality standards

Developing quality programs requires:
- knowing the customer's needs and desires

- understanding how to meet those needs/wants

- determining performance measurements

- exceeding the customer's needs/expectations

Maurice Rasgon is the Export Manager of Blue Cross Beauty Products, Inc., a cosmetic business based in San Fernando, California. Blue Cross has about 110 employees and markets its products in Australia, Europe and South America. Mr. Rasgon makes the point that quality is absolutely necessary to assure repeat sales in international markets. And as he says: "We are out of business if we only sell someone once. Repeat sales are lifeblood of our overall international marketing efforts."

He notes that global quality standards vary from country to country and adds: "The Japanese are exceptionally quality-conscious. When we sell in Japan, we have an agreement with them that if the order contains more than 1% defective items, they have the right to reject the entire order. That's a high quality standard, but we try to maintain this benchmark regardless where we do business."

Meeting Specifications in a timely manner

Fiona Taylor, the owner of Uniglobe Research Corporation based in Los Angeles, does international business in blood supplies. She says: "Quality means that material we ship must meet the specifications of the end user. Anything else is unacceptable. We also find it is essential to let customers know if there is going to be a delay. Sometimes they will wait, but if you leave them in the dark, they'll never call again. Promptness is important. For example, a customer may ask for samples from several suppliers. If our samples arrive first and meet their specifications, they probably won't bother to check out the others. I also think it is important to meet clients face to face at least once a year. They appreciate the effort of you visiting them even if you do not have a real business on that particular day and it definitely helps you to build a long term relationship with your counterparts."

Quality is everyone's responsibility

Achieving consistent quality is one of the biggest challenges facing small businesses. Quality has to be taken seriously from top to bottom of the company and must become everyone's mantra.

Joseph Martin, Operations Manager of Bobrick Inc, a plumbing supplies firm in North Hollywood that does significant international business in Australia, Singapore and Saudi Arabia, defines quality as "providing the customer with a product that is functioning, a product that meets both of the customers and our standards. Quality is a product that does not have installation or performance problems, and it serves the purpose for which it is meant."

Joseph gave the analogy of traveling by plane and said: "We have products that meet various customer needs. It's sort of like getting on a plane. You have economy, business, and first class. In 'first class' we have a registered, patented product that nobody else can make. Our 'business class' product is less exclusive, and our 'economy class' is more basic. We have several quality levels, but at each level we strive to have our product comply with the highest quality. And we stand hundred percent behind them. If there is any problem we fix or replace the product."

Total quality management

Quality can be achieved through ownership and responsibility of all of the employees. Bob Amudsen, Export

Manager of Card Key, emphasized quality accountability standards in his company and said: "We treat the product internally with a customer-supplier relationship as it moves through the production process. The person receiving the product has a quality expectation as to the state the product should be in when he/she receives it. So in addition to the company's inspection processes, our firm creates an empowering mind set among all employees, so that they too become inspectors. The company wants them to take pride in what they do, and so in most stages of manufacturing, they are either obliged to; or have the option of stamping the work with their initials in confirmation of their own contribution. When the product goes to final production stage, we ship it with a small summation sheet that includes the stamps of all the employees who participated in the manufacturing process."

ISO-9000 Requirements

The U.S. Government provides a series of five ISO documents: ISO-9000, 9001, 9002, 9003 and 9004, which provide guidance on selection and implementation of an appropriate quality management program/system for your operation.

The purpose of the ISO 9000 series is to document, implement, and demonstrate the quality assurance system used by companies that supply goods and services internationally.

ISO standards are required to be reviewed every five years; information on the status of these reviews can be obtained from the American Society for Quality Control: http://www.ASQ.org.

There are three ways for a manufacturer to prove compliance with the requirements of one of the ISO standards:

- Manufacturers may evaluate their quality control system and self-declare their conformance to one of the ISO 9000 quality standards.

- Second party evaluations may be required by some foreign buyers who conduct their own, and these evaluations are mandatory only for companies wishing to become a supplier to that particular buyer.

- Third-party quality system evaluations and registrations may be voluntary or mandatory and are conducted by persons or organizations independent of either supplier or buyer.

As conformity to the ISO 9000 standards becomes recognized and required by foreign and domestic buyers, it can be used as a strong marketing tool. Therefore, it is crucial for manufacturers to determine their buyer's position on ISO-9000 requirements.

For further information on U.S., foreign and international voluntary standards, government regulations, and rules of certification for non-agricultural products, contact the National Center for Standards and Certification Information (NCSCI): http://www.nist.gov/ncsci.

TEAMWORK

Globalization enhances the importance of teamwork

Your competitors can copy and own every advantage you have in terms of quality, pricing and packaging. The only things they cannot duplicate are your team members, associates and employees.

Owners, managers and other top executives must encourage teamwork so that the company can tap into the diverse experiences and knowledge of their employees and benefit from them in problem solving, improved performance, and developing innovative products.

The Card Key Company, which manufactures access keys, developed a peer awards program that was organized by the employees themselves without the involvement of upper or middle management in any way. The operating body is a committee of seven or eight employees who meet at least bi-monthly to consider the merits of employee suggestions. The person whose suggestion is judged to be the best receives the top monetary reward, and these awards are perceived to be more meaningful since they come from a peer group.

In today's fiercely competitive global marketplace, the manager who utilizes "soft assets" such as knowledge, experience, creativity, imagination and talent of all of his associates and employees has a distinct advantage. Delegating responsibility and decision-making often result in better products and services. Toyota is an example of a company that thrives on employees inputs. Every year, the company receives over two million suggestions from its employees, which accounts to almost 60 ideas per employee. Toyota implements a majority of them in some form or another. Each suggestion aimed at reducing cost and improving the company's business practices and profitability receives a monetary award based on its value to the organization. Furthermore, the implementation of one's suggestion enhances employee self-esteem.

CUSTOMER SATISFACTION

Global business has several different types of customers:

- End-users.
- Intermediate customers – they are middlemen such as distributors and dealers.
- Multi-national customers – these customers often have different habits, preferences, expectations and cultural values. When companies go global, they cannot rely on instantaneous harmony and mutual understanding; showing cultural sensitivity and awareness is absolutely essential in dealing with foreign customers.

British Airways, which has more international customers than any other airline, always strives to take the cultural characteristics of their customers into consideration. Bob Ayling, former CEO of British Airways, focused on a marketing plan with an international touch. The plan helps employees understand the global vision of the company. As he says: "We don't want to ram our Britishness down people's throats. There is no more Empire. We are just a small nation on an offshore island to make our way in the world."

As a visible expression of its global outlook, British Airways uses African murals, Japanese calligraphy, and

Scottish tartan plaids on its ticket jackets, cabin crew scarves, business cards, and even on the tail of its planes.

Customer-Centeredness

The biggest challenge in global marketing is to tailor your products and services to the different cultures, climates, and regulatory environments of your customers. Degremont, a French water treatment company, has purification plants in 40 countries and has been growing 15% annually. The company attributes its outstanding growth to understanding the exact needs of each of the countries it serves, and to adapting its products to meet those specific needs. In China, for instance, the needs range from facilities for creating drinking water to sewage treatment plants and technology for toxic waste clean up.

Global customer service

Focusing on customer service with cultural awareness pays big dividends in the retention of foreign clients. The guidelines for effective customer service are similar to domestic ones:

- Personal attention – Customers want to feel that they are treated as human beings. The old adage is universal and definitely applicable in international business as well: "Customers don't care what you know until they know that you care."

- Dependability – Staff members dealing directly with customers should be competent enough to satisfy customer needs and expectations.

- Promptness – Customers not only want quality products/services, they want it quickly.

- Employee Competence – Customers must be convinced that employees who are performing the service have a superior level of knowledge.

Some additional international customer service tips:

- Make sure your operation runs smoothly and can deliver the customer's demand before you make any commitment to your foreign buyers.

- Provide detailed handbooks that outline your product's features, selling points, your brands benefits to distributors, agents, licensees and venture partners.

- You need a support line for technical questions and complaints.

- Supply product warranties with sales to your clients.

- Put together customer policies and procedures, including payment methods, discount and terms, insurance, advertising/sales promotion and granting exclusive representation.

- Establish clear reporting guidelines for both export staff and support departments such as manufacturing, engineering, finance and credit.

INNOVATION

"The great prerequisite for the prosperous management of ordinary business is the want of imagination."

- *William Hazlitt, 1806*

The next opportunities won't be based merely on low-cost labor, but on "innovation and strategy". Today, companies cannot rely on past successes. They must constantly produce improved and innovative products and services that meet customer needs. Small businesses are poised to respond to these challenges because they are not encumbered by the layers of bureaucracy and administrative clutter. They can act much faster than their large competitors. And since the leaders of small businesses are more in touch with all of their employees, they are in a better position to get the best out of them to draw on their intellectual power, innovative spirit, knowledge and experience.

Turning on creativity

Businesses need to create a climate of constructive conflict – an environment that fosters creativity and innovation. Here are some tips on how you can generate innovative spirit in your business:

- Question your success. Do not rely on assumptions and beliefs. Encourage open debate and feedback from every employee. Be flexible and open minded when change is needed.

- Employ people with creative potential. Give all of your employees a chance to express their views and treat every idea as a potential source of future innovation.

- Brainstorm. This technique is a structured method of getting the largest number of ideas from a group in a non-judgmental way. All ideas are welcomed and none are considered as too "far out." Once all ideas have been brought forward, evaluate them in terms of their pluses and minuses and determine overall viability for your business. Brainstorm involves every member of the organization and sometimes the best ideas come from the least likely sources. There are many examples of blockbuster ideas coming from the receptionist or a secretary, or even from the mail room. The reason is that ideas from these sources often tend to be unbiased and sometimes original. Since the purpose behind brainstorming is to produce a large volume of ideas, don't stop until you have at least fifty.

- Hold regular meetings with your sales people and field engineers who have close contact with customers. They have a wealth of first-hand knowledge about competition, product development, changing market demands, trends and customer expectations.

Managing Change

Employees are generally resistant if change is forced on them from the top down. Change can be more effectively implemented when employees have been brought into the big picture and shown how their contributions will lead to achieving positive results in the firm.

If you are thinking of instituting major changes in your organization, here are some tips to consider:

- Involve your employees actively in the process of change. If there is resistance, maintain open communications and encourage employees to express their problems without fears.

- Include incentive packages in your planning stage for change.

- Move quickly!

- If re-training is required, provide it, and encourage employees to learn by doing.

- Give regular support and feedback and let them know how the planned changes are progressing.

- Create an environment that welcomes change. Staff meetings and seminars are good techniques to promote the free-flowing exchange of ideas.

Learning from your mistakes

Sometimes change prompts a "disaster" that can also teach a valuable lesson to the parties involved. Coca-Cola is a great example; in the 1980's, Coke was losing its market share to Pepsi-Cola. So Coke researched and developed a new sweeter Coke, which was called New Coke. However, the sales of their core product (later to be renamed Classic Coke) increased while the sales of New Coke failed to take off. In short, New Coke was a "marketing failure." Roberto Goizuetta, who was then the Chief Executive Officer of Coca-

Cola, said that "New Coke made us realize that Coca-Cola was more than a flavor or a bottle. It was a mental attitude." So this "marketing tragedy" became a valuable lesson in the enduring value of the original core brand.

GLOBAL LEADERSHIP

"Today and in the 21st century, management's ability to transform the organization and its people into a global company is a prerequisite for survival because both its customers and competitors have become cosmopolitan."

Kenichi Ohmae, Beyond National Borders

Increased competition in the international marketplace and globalization has put the need of effective global leaders at the forefront. Leaders must communicate well and show they are open to people in all countries, and that they can successfully engage in international alliances to commit their firms to long-term business opportunities, and that through this process they can find and celebrate the shared values with all the stakeholders.

This particular approach was implemented by Ritz Carlton at its new hotel in Shanghai, China and underscored its main management philosophy of global culture. Ritz Carlton took over the property under its own name in the late 1990's with a local staff of around 1000 people. The management of Ritz Carlton chain prides itself on legendary customer service and impeccable quality standards decided a comprehensive transformation and management of the new hotel in Shanghai.

They started the make-over of the hotel from the employee's quarters as opposed to the main lobby. The reasons were twofold: firstly, to demonstrate and have the employees feel sharp improvement and overall enhancement of services; secondly, the employees are the crown jewel of their stakeholders in the company. This gesture of thoughtfulness and yet very powerful approach helped the company to relay their paramount global culture to their employees: "We are Ladies and Gentlemen Serving Ladies and Gentlemen".

The management of a global business requires symbolic and effective actions, which has tremendous impact on minimizing differences and helping stakeholders, employees, customers and suppliers to integrate into global culture.

Future global business success depends on developing effective global leaders who are aware of opportunities and exploiting them to grow and expand their influence around the globe.

Given the fact that the average product cycle of goods today is 10-18 months as opposed to five or more years in the past, responding promptly to the needs of the fast-paced marketplace and constant change is absolutely critical for the survival of any business. Leaders have to expand their duties of being performer and operator of current business to becoming an effective and skilled agent of change.

Leaders have to recognize that they need to be co-leaders of their team in helping the organization to navigate successfully through turbulent and competitive times. They have to act like a coach to have their employees embrace and implement their global vision and work closely with potential international champions that can assist them in expanding their company's global presence.

Leaders should adopt an operation style of "management by traveling around." Small business owners need to visit foreign customers and their facilities at least once a year. These are not just "courtesy" visits consisting of sitting in the office having coffee and chatting with their counterparts. They have to go out to the shop floor and observe the manufacturing in process and talk to the workers to see how they can be of further help in maintaining their business.

Learning must be an integral part of executive duties in small and mid-sized companies. Regular fact-finding visits to customers can contribute to acquiring valuable information in developing innovative products and helping your company stay competitive.

GLOBAL BUSINESS PLAN

Products/Services

Step 1: Select the most exportable products to be sold in international markets.

The product has to meet the needs of the buyer in terms of price, value to the customer/country and market demand.

What is your product line?

1._____

2._____

3._____

What products have the best potential for international trade?

1._____

2._____

3._____

Step 2: Evaluate the products that can be offered internationally.

What makes your products unique for an overseas market?
1._____

2._____

3._____

Why will international buyers purchase the products from your company?

1._____

2._____

3._____

How much inventory will be necessary to sell overseas?

1._____

2._____

3._____

Industry Analysis

Step 1.   Determine your industry's growth for the next 3 years.

Contact the people in the same business or industry, read and research industry-specific magazines, attend trade fairs and seminars.

_____

_____

_____

Step 2: Research how competitive your industry is in the global market.

Use the National Trade Data Bank (NTDB), obtain import/export statistics from the Bureau of Census and contact the U.S. Small Business Administration (SBA) or the U.S. Department of Commerce (DOC) district office in your area.

_____

_____

_____

Step 3: Find out your industry's future growth in the international market.

Contact the SBA or the U.S. Foreign & Commercial Service (US & FCS) district office, and contact a DOC country or industry desk in Washington D.C.

_____

_____

_____

Step 4: Research federal or state government market studies that have been conducted in your industry's potential international markets.

Contact SBA, your state international trade office, a DOC country or industry desk in Washington D.C.

_____

_____

_____

Step 5: Find export data available in your industry.

Contact your SBA or DOC district office.

_____

_____

_____

Business/Company Analysis

Step 1: Why is your business successful in the domestic market? What's your growth rate?

_____

_____

_____

Step 2: What products do you feel have export potential?

_____

_____

_____

Step 3: What are the competitive advantages of your products or business over other domestic and international business?

_____

_____

_____

Marketing Your Product

Given the market potential for your products in international markets, how is your product unique?

1. What are your product's advantages?

_____

_____

_____

2. What are your product's disadvantages?

_____

_____

_____

3. What are the competitive product's advantages?

_____

_____

_____

4. What are the competitive product's disadvantages?

_____

_____

_____

What are the needs that will be filled by your product in a foreign market?

_____

_____

What competitive products are sold abroad and to whom?

_____

_____

How complex is your product? What skill or special training is required To:

1. Install your product?

_____

_____

2. Use your product?

_____

_____

3. Maintain your product?

_____

_____

4. Service your product?

_____

_____

What options and Accessories are Available?

1. Has an aftermarket been developed for your product?

_____

_____

2. What other equipment does the buyer need to use your product?

_____

_____

3. What complementary goods does your product require?

_____

_____

If your product is an industrial good:

1. What firms are likely to use it?

    _____

    _____

2. What is the useful lifespan of your product?

    _____

    _____

3. Is use of life affected by climate? If so, How?

    _____

    _____

4. Will geography affect product purchase? For example, transportation problems?

    _____

    _____

If the product is a consumer good:

1. Who will consume it? How frequently will the product be bought?

_____

_____

2. Is consumption affected by climate?

_____

_____

3. Is consumption affected by geography? For example, transportation problems?

_____

_____

4. Will the product be restricted abroad for example tariffs, quotas or non-tariff barriers?

_____

_____

5. Does your product conflict with traditions, habits or beliefs of customers abroad?

_____

_____

Step 1: Select the best countries to market your product.
The U.S. Small Business Administration and the United States Foreign Commercial Service may be of assistance in providing product market analysis. Preliminary screening involves defining the physical, political, economic and cultural environment. Rate the following factors in each category.

1. Select two countries you think have the best market potential for your product.
2. Review the market factors for each country.
3. Research data/information for each country.
4. Rate each factor on a scale of 1-5 with 5 being the best.
5. Select a target market country on your ratings.

What is the projected growth rates of the two countries selected over the next 3-5 years?

_____

_____

Step 2: Determine projected sales levels

What is your present U.S. market share (percentage)?

_____

_____

What are the projected sales for similar products in your chosen international markets for the future?

_____

_____

What sales volume will you project for your products in these international markets for the coming year?

_____

_____

What is the projected growth in these international markets over the next five years?

_____

_____

Step 3: Identify Customers in Your Chosen Markets

What companies, agents or distributors have purchased the products?

_____

_____

What companies, agents or distributors have made recent requests for information on similar products?

_____

_____

What companies, agents or distributors would most likely be prospective customers for your export products?

_____

_____

Step 4: Determine Methods of Exporting

How do other U.S. firms sell in the markets you have chosen?

Will you sell direct to the customer?

    1. Who will represent your firm?

_____

_____

2. Who will service the customer's needs?

_____

_____

Step 5: Building a Distributor or Agent Relationship

Will you appoint an agent or distributor to handle your export market?

1. What facilities does the agent or distributor need to service the markct?

_____

_____

2. What type of client should your agent or distributor is familiar with in order to sell your product?

_____

_____

3. What territory should the agent or distributor cover?

_____

_____

4. What financial strength should the agent or distributor have?

_____

_____

5. What other competitive or non-competitive lines are acceptable for the agent or distributor to carry?

_____

_____

6. How many sales representatives does the agent or distributor need and how often will they cover the territory?

_____

_____

Will you use an export management company to do your marketing and distribution?

YES   NO

If yes, have you developed an acceptable sales and marketing plan with realistic goals you can agree to?

YES   NO

Comments:

_____

_____

Support Functions

Step 1: Identify product concerns.

Can the potential buyer see a functioning model or sample of your product that is substantially the same as would be received from production?

YES   NO

Comments:

_____

_____

What product labeling requirements must be met? (Metric measurements, AC or DC electrical, voltage, etc) The European Community now requires three languages on all new packaging.

_____

_____

When and how can product conversion requirements be obtained?

_____

_____

Can products be delivered on time as ordered?

YES   NO

Comments:

_____

_____

Step 2: Identify literature concerns.

If required, will you have literature in language other than English?

YES   NO

Do you need a product literature translator to handle the technical language?

YES NO

What special concerns should be addressed in sales literature to ensure quality and informative representation of your product?

_____

_____

Step 3: Identify customer relations concerns.

What is the delivery time and methods of shipment?

_____

_____

What are payment terms?

_____

_____

What are the warranty terms?

_____

_____

Who will service the product when needed?

_____

_____

How will you communicate with your customer?

_____

_____

Are you prepared to give the same order and delivery preferences to your international customers that you give to your domestic customers?

YES NO

Marketing Strategy

In international sales, the chosen "terms of sale" are the most important. Where should you make the product available at your plant: at the port of exit, landed at the port of importation or delivered free and clear to the customer's door? The answer to this question involves determining what the market requires, and how much risk you are willing to take.

Pricing strategy depends on "Terms of Sale" and also value added services of bringing the product to the international market.

Step 1: Define International Pricing Strategy

How do you calculate the price for each product?

_____

_____

What factors have you considered in setting prices?

_____

_____

Which products' sales are very sensitive to price changes?

_____

_____

How important is pricing in your overall marketing strategy?

_____

_____

What are your discount policies?

_____

_____

What terms of sales are best for your export product?

_____

_____

Step 2: Define promotional strategy

What advertising materials will you use?

_____

_____

What trade shows or trade missions will you participate in, if any?

_____

_____

What time of year and how often will foreign travel is made to customer markets?

_____

_____

Step 3: Define customer services

What special customer services do you offer?

_____

_____

What types of payment options do you offer?

_____

_____

How do you handle a customer's merchandise return?

_____

_____

Bibliography

A Basic Guide to Exporting, U.S. Department of Commerce in Cooperation of Federal Express Corporation, 1992

Acuff L. Frank, "How to Negotiate with Anyone Anywhere", Amacom 1993

Asian Development Outlook 2003

Axtell Roger E., The Do's and Taboos of International Trade, New York: John Wiley & Sons 1989

Breaking Into the Trade Game: A Small Business Guide to Exporting, U.S. Small Business Administration and AT& T

Business Week, "It was a Hit in Buenos Aires-So Why Not Boise:" September 7, 1998

Caslione A. John, Thomas R. Andrew "Global Destiny", Dearborn Publishing Company 2002

Czinkota Michael R., Ilkka A Ronkainen, Martha Ortiz, The Export Marketing Imperative, Thomson Publishing 2004

Copeland Lennie and Lewis Griggs, Going International, New York: Random House, 1985

Dalton Maxine, Ernst Chris, Deal Jennifer, Leslie Jean, "Success for the Global Manager, Jossey-Bass 2002

Entrepreneurs, Economic Forum 1999

Export America, September 2001

Gupta Anil, Govindarajan. "The Quest for Global Dominance", Jossey Bass 2008

Garten Jeffrey E, "The Big Ten" Basic Books, 1997

Harris Philip, Moran Robert, Moran Sarah, "Managing cultural Differences, Elsevier Butterworth, 2004

Hodge Sheida, "Global Smarts" John Wiley & Sons, Inc 2000

Hodgson James Day, Sana Yoshiro, Graham L. John, "Doing Business with the New Japan" Rowman & Littlefield Publishers, Inc 2000

Johnson E. Thomas, Export/Import-Procedures & Documentation

Julie R. Weeks, International Trade Opens New Doors for Women
Mahbubani, "The New Asian Hemisphere"

Martin Jeannette, Chaney Lillian, "Global Business Etiquette" Praeger, 2006

Moran Robert, Harris R. Philip, Stripp G. William, "Developing the Global Organization, Gulf Publishing Company 1993

Ohmae, Kenichi, The Borderless World, New York: Harper Business, 1990

Requejo Hernandez William and Graham L. John, "Global Negotiation the New Rules" Palgrave Macmillan 2008

Rosen Robert, "Global Literacy's", Simon and Shuster 2000
Rossman L. Marlene, "The International Businesswoman of the 1990's, Praeger Publisher 1990

Stanat Ruth, Chris West, Global Jumpstart, Perseus Books 1999
Successful Business Leadership 25th May 2008

Wall Street Journal, "Making Yourself Understood in Beijing", July 17, 2008

Wells L. Fargo and Karin B Dulat, Exporting From Start to Finance, New York: McGraw-Hill, 1996

Wilfong James and Toni Seger, Taking Your Business Global, New Jersey: Career Press 1997

Book Order Form

Ultimate Trade LLC
5334 Lindley Ave. Ste.324
Encino, Ca 91316
Phone: 818-609-9196
Fax: 818-708-9571

$_____Subtotal of books ($14.99 each)
+_____Shipping and Handling
        ($1.50 per item)
+_____Tax (California residents add 8.25%)
$_____Total

Send check or money order (no cash or COD's)

Name_____

Address_____

City_____State_____

Zip Code_____

Please allow 2 weeks for delivery

HOW TO HELP YOUR TEAM BECOME GLOBAL

Keynote presentations

Let author Ayse Oge personally inspire and empower your organization, educational institution, team or conference attendees. A keynote with Ayse is informative, entertaining and aimed at generating excitement, shifting attitudes and maximizing performance.

What others are saying about Ayse's presentations:

On behalf of all the participants of Mount St. Mary College, I would like to thank you for your presentation. Your insights were appreciated in presenting the material. The participants commended on the high level of your presentation, knowledge and ability to transfer a vast amount of information in such a short period of time.
Peter H. Antoniou
Professor, Mount St. Mary College

We thank you for your participation in the 3rd Annual Global California Conference as a panelist and presenting "Global Branding" topic to our International Trade professionals. Your presentation was an important part of the conference's success.
Tony Livoti
Monterey Bay International Trade Association (MBITA)

Your dynamic presentation about negotiation and multi-cultural skills strengthened audience's knowledge about essential skills for success in international business. They

really appreciated many real life examples that you shared with them.
Maria Keller, EMBA
Instructor, UCLA

Thank you for your wonderful presentation. The audience enjoyed hearing about Going Global and your experiences.
Candy Hansen
President, San Joaquin Valley International Trade Association Workshops

"Go Global to Win", series designed to assist prospective and/or seasoned exporters in the development of the skills associated with successful exporting. These workshops are highly interactive and customized to your team's environment and challenges.

"Go Global to Win" Audio Four CD Set
Many people won't take the time to read an entire book, but they will listen to an audio program. Audio set focuses on real life examples for exporters and comes with a bonus material from author Ayse Oge not included in the book.

For more information on keynotes and workshops or to order products, contact us at

E-mail: Oge@earthlink.net
Phone: 818-609-9196
Fax: 818-708-9571
www.goglobaltowin.com